NO NIGHT THERE

Devotional Sermons
by
The Rev. Murdoch Campbell, M.A.

Because thou hast been my help, therefore in the shadow of thy wings will I rejoice. (Psalm 63, v. 7)

Published by
The Religious Bookshop
Stornoway, Isle of Lewis

CONTENTS

FOREWORD

The devotional writings of Rev. Murdoch Campbell are too well known now to need any introduction. He works a vein of deep religious devotion which makes an appeal to spiritually-minded and mature believers, exercised in Christian faith and experience. These sermons have an aura of the inner sanctuary about them, and as the title of the book indicates, a title taken from one of the sermons published here, the outlook is mostly towards heaven. One is impressed with Mr Campbell's grasp of Scripture. The sermons quote lavishly from the Word of God; they are essentially Bibline, which, after all, is the glory of sermons which proclaim what God says and not man's opinions. This little volume is sure of a welcome wherever a warm spirit of devotion to the Lord and Saviour exists.

(Rev.) James W. Fraser,
Free North Church, Inverness.

THE SECRET OF ETERNAL PEACE

"*Acquaint now thyself with Him, and be at peace: thereby good shall come unto Thee*"–Job, Ch. 22, v. 21

These words of Eliphaz the Temanite may imply that he did not really believe that Job knew the Lord, and that, if he did, God would not have subjected him to the great trials through which, at that hour, he was passing. If he had been truly acquainted with the Almighty he would have lived in peace and would have continued to enjoy, within the sphere of providence, the favour and goodness of God to the end. But Job did know the Lord, savingly and personally. It was he who uttered the immortal words: "For I know that my Redeemer liveth." He was a man who, beyond all his contemporaries, bore God's image both in his life and in his conduct in this world. He also had peace with God through His Redeemer; and the Lord, the source of all real good, was truly the Portion of his soul. The severe trial of his faith was, indeed, one true evidence that the Lord loved him. "Whom the Lord loveth He chasteneth and scourgeth every son whom He receiveth."

In offering a few comments on these words I should, however, like to deal with them in their wider context and application. They speak to us all. Do they not proclaim that God does desire the acquaintance of men that He might bless them with eternal peace and with the good part that shall never be taken from them?

There are three thoughts which confront us in this verse. There is:

I. Man's Great Privilege–"Acquaint now thyself with Him".

Then we have:

II. The Great Promise given to all who, by His grace, avail themselves of this privilege–"And be at peace: thereby good shall come unto thee".

Lastly we have:

III. The Opportune hour which is expressed in the word "NOW".

First of all, then, let us consider:

I. Man's great privilege

How unspeakably wonderful are the kindness and condescension of God when He desires to know and to befriend sinful men and women whose feet are in the dust and whose hearts are full of sin. It is, indeed, a great wonder that He should look on any mere creature in the Creation. "The Lord is high above all nations, and His glory above the heavens. Who is like unto the Lord our God who dwelleth on High, who humbleth himself to behold the things that are in heaven and in the earth." (Ps. 113.)

To all who come to know Him as their everlasting Friend and Redeemer this is a wonder that shall continue to deepen within their beings throughout the ages to come. The Bible, which is an infallible revelation of God's mind to men, tells us that before the universe was brought into existence the "delights" of Christ were with the sons of men. He rejoiced in the prospect of inhabiting our fallen world and in having His tabernacle with men. And we know who Christ was: He was the Eternal Son of God, the Second Person in the Godhead. He was to come where we are that we might come to know Him, and that we might dwell with Him for ever in another world of unspeakable blessedness.

The great end for which God created man was that he might both glorify Him and enjoy Him for ever. Adam in his original state of holiness walked with God as with a Friend. Between him and his Maker there was perfect harmony of mind and will. Alas, this acquaintance and mutual communion only lasted for a brief hour. He, the natural and federal head of mankind, through Satan's lie, wilfully and with his eyes open, sinned against God. God then, in all justice, left him. He lost communion with Him. He turned to be God's enemy. The poison which penetrated through his being from the fangs of Satan produced an enmity toward God within his heart, and within the heart of all who descended from him by ordinary generation. This is expressed in the previous chapter. "They say unto God, depart from us; for we desire not the knowledge of thy ways." These are among the most evil, the most foolish, and the most terrible words that man ever uttered in the presence of God. And did God finally and for ever depart from man? Did He, as in the case of the angels who kept not their first estate, leave man, as he deserved, to perish in his sin? Did He cease from seeking any further acquaintance with men who had come under His displeasure? No. God asked Adam the solemn question, "Where art thou?" Man in his shame, and shivering in his guilt, was trying to hide himself from the One before whose eyes all things are open and naked. Then came the awe inspiring moment when God, in infinite mercy and sovereign grace, brought to light His Way of Salvation through "the seed of the woman" who was to come in the fulness of time to rescue and redeem men from the peril and power of evil. He alone could bruise the head of the serpent, satisfy God in His law and justice, and bring us back into a new and lasting acquaintance with Himself. This, indeed, is one of the great themes of God's Holy Word, without the knowledge of which it is impossible to have any true acquaintance with God.

When Christ, the Incarnate and Personal Word, appeared in this world, God's eyes rested on Him with infinite delight. They still do, and ever shall. If our eyes rest upon the same Person, as our Saviour and Righteousness, then we shall come to know God. God delights in those who delight in His well-beloved Son. This is how our acquaintance with God is for ever established. "No man cometh unto the Father but by me." "If a man love Me, he will keep my words and we will come unto Hime, and make our abode with him." To dwell with God is to know God and to love God.

There is another aspect of this acquaintance with God which we must emphasise. One end for which Christ gives His people His Spirit is that He might enlighten them in the knowledge of Himself. This means that only God can acquaint us with God. When Simon Peter, in answer to Christ's question as to who He was, made the great confession that He was the Christ, the Son of the Living God, our Lord told him that his knowledge of Him was given him by God the Father through the Holy Spirit. "He shall glorify me, for he shall receive of mine and shall show it unto you." This acquaintance then, which flows from God in the Three Persons and which has it s source in His sovereign love and will, is wholly outwith the reach of the creature. "No man hath seen God at any time; the only Son who is in the bosom of the Father He hath revealed Him."

The means which God's Spirit uses in bringing us to know Christ are the Scriptures and the Throne of Grace. The Bible is a perfect mirror in which we see both the sufferings and the glory of the Redeemer. This was the witness of the Spirit in the Word from the beginning. The Incarnate Word is present in the written word. "Search the Scriptures for in them ye think ye have eternal life and these are they which testify of me." While God's eternal power and Godhead are manifested in His creation and providence, it is pre-eminently in the Scriptures that His grace and love are revealed. In the Bible we have a progressive revelation of God's interest in men, and of His desire that they might come to know Him as the only living and true God. Those who fail to see Him in His Word seldom, if ever, see Him or find Him anywhere else. The vast majority of the human race who are ignorant of the Gospel either deny His existence or they make idolatrous and silly "gods" in their own image.

A saving acquaintance with God also comes through prayer. The Holy Spirit is the Spirit of grace and of supplications. "Ye have an unction from the Holy One and ye know all things." "Open thou mine eyes," prayed the Psalmist, "that I may behold wondrous things out of Thy law." Many of God's people could tell of blessed seasons in their life when God graciously fulfilled His promise to them. "Draw nigh to God and He will draw nigh to you." It was in the act of prayer and in a state of penitence that the publican came to know God. It was then that Christ extended to his soul the sceptre of His grace, and he went down to his house justified and forgiven–the subject of God's mercy. His promise is that if we come and reason with Him at the Throne of Grace He will send us on our way rejoicing with our crimson and scarlet sins for ever washed away in the precious blood of His dear Son. Two dear friends of mine, now, I believe, with Christ in their eternal home, used to tell of the hour when Christ revealed Himself to their souls in answer to prayer. With their hearts full of wonder and heads bowed all they could say was: "My Lord and My God." They had come to know Him who loved them from all eternity.

Nothing is more real to the spiritual man than this holy converse with the Eternal. The Bible speaks of men and women from the beginning of time who, by faith, became acquainted with God. "Enoch walked with

God." For three hundred years this man was in constant enjoyment of God's presence till God translated him to his happy Home above. The Lord spoke of Abraham as His friend, "Abraham my friend." It was at Bethel that Jacob enjoyed God's presence and heard His voice. God embraced him in His promise. It was an hour which marked a deepening of his acquaintance with the Angel of the Covenant. "The God who fed me all my life long unto this day." These were among his last words. Another of the saints spoke of God as ever holding him by the hand. "Nevertheless I am continually with Thee; Thou hast holden me by my right hand." (Ps. 73.) How appropriately does Paul express this experimental knowledge of God as his Saviour, Preserver and Friend. "I know whom I have believed, and I am persuaded that He is able to keep that which I have committed unto Him against that day." There is not in the Bible a more wonderful and a more detailed description of Christ than that given by His Bride, the Church, in her Song. "This is my Beloved: and this is my Friend." "He is altogether lovely." The blind, graceless daughters of Jerusalem had never seen Him with their eyes. If our acquaintance with God is as real as it was in the lives of such a people then we are their spiritual contempories, and we have the same promise that one day we shall see Him as He is.

Now notice:

II. God's great promise—to all who are given this Privilege.

The promise is two-fold. There is the promise of "peace" and there is the promise of "good". Christ is spoken of in the Scriptures as the Prince of Peace. In other words He is the Giver and the Source of true and everlasting peace. He exercises a threefold office, and through each of these His peace is communicated to the soul. There is the peace which comes through His death, or through His offering up of Himself as our Great High Priest. "And having made pace through the blood of His Cross, by Him to reconcile all things unto Himself . . . whether they be things in earth or things in heaven." When on the Cross He cried, "It is finished", the veil of the temple was rent in twain. With the blood of sprinkling He entered into the presence of God for us and obtained our eternal redemption and reconciliation. This is where the attributes of God in the work of redemption all rest. "He shall rest in His love and rejoice over thee with singing." (Zephaniah 3.) It is through the sprinkling of His blood that we enter into peace with God—that peace of mind and conscience "which passeth all understanding". Many of us remember the hour when by faith we looked to the Lamb of God, and knew that through His merits and righteousness our sins were cast forever into the sea of God's forgiveness and removed from us as far as east is distant from the west. "They shall be remembered no more."

And there is a peace which comes to us through His prophetic office—or through His Word. "Peace be still." "For He will speak peace unto His people, and to His saints." God the Father gave Him the "tongue of the learned that He might know how to speak a word in season to him that is weary." "Thou wilt keep him in perfect peace whose mind is stayed on

Thee because he trusteth in Thee." "Great peace have they who love Thy law and nothing shall offend them." Do you, child of God, not remember when, like a restless dove, your weary sin-striken soul reposed in His bosom and when a word from His lips composed your spirit? "Return unto thy rest, O, my soul: for the Lord hath dealt bountifully with thee." "My peace I give unto you." In heaven our rest shall be eternal and perfect. "There remaineth therefore a rest to the people of God." (Heb. 4.)

We are living in a restless and perilous age. Our personal providences, also, may often be the sources of our disquiet; but, "Be still and know that I am God", He who is our Great High Priest, and the One by whose word we are nourished and sustained from day to day, is also our Eternal King who rules in His Providence and also over the vast dominions of His creation. "There is none like unto the God of Jeshurun who rideth upon the heaven in thy help . . . the Eternal God is thy refuge and underneath are the everlasting arms." This peace, then, is His precious blessing to all who, conscious of their many needs and sins, come to Him who alone is our help.

You may, perhaps, be asking yourself the question which sometimes brings disquiet to some of God's people—"How shall it fare with me at last in the swellings of Jordan?" But the Lord, dear friend, assures us that when we pass through the waters He shall be with us, and though the rivers they shall not overflow us.

"Mark thou the perfect and behold
The man of uprightness;
Because that surely of this man
The latter end is peace."

God's peace is united to another great blessing—the blessing of true "good". "Thereby shall good come unto thee." Here we are confronted with man's greatest folly and tragedy—his utter ignorance of what real or true good is. In this we see how deeply Satan has deceived him and how sin has so disastrously ensnared him. He is allured from the ways of peace and from the goodness of God by a false and empty *mirage* which is eternally divorced from reality.

There are many, as we know, who think of good in terms of material possessions. Our Lord solemnly warns us against this when He says: "What shall it profit a man if he shall gain the whole world and lose his own soul?" In one of His parables He speaks of a rich farmer who was but a poor "fool". He was a man who had done well in this world. He had, as he thought, "much goods laid up for many years". He would now draw in his chair and enjoy life. He had evidently no feeling of ill-health and no expectation of death. Then it happened. Death came to his door. He heard a voice. "But God said unto him, thou fool, this night *thy soul* shall be required of thee, then whose shall those things be which thou has provided?" In a moment he found himself in a place of unending despair, destitution and deprivation. This man had no awareness that his real self was primarily his *soul* and not his physical life, and that, therefore, mere *things* were utterly irrelevant to his deeper needs and remote from his eternal welfare. He thought he had "good" and "security", but neither was his. In the words of the Psalmist, man without God "shall carry nothing hence", and is like "the beasts which perish". Is he not really worse than the beasts? With them death is the end, but with such a man it is a beginning without an end in a lost eternity but still of conscious existence.

In another parable our Lord speaks of a man who lived in so-called pleasures, having, what so many speak of today, "a good time". He drank with his false friends in sin, and satisfied his sinful lusts at the unclean cisterns of this world. God had no place in all his thoughts, and God's cause and people he ignored–Lazarus, for example–as of no consequence. "And in hell he lifted up his eyes." His was also a sudden transition from carnal pleasure to perdition, from drink to damnation, from the dance to his doom where he shall for ever remember and weep over his folly. "Son, remember."

There is, dear friend, only one real good. It is God himself. This is what our Lord meant when He commended Mary's choice. "There is but one thing needful and Mary hath chosen the good part that shall never be taken from her." These words imply that death can snatch from us every gift and favour except One. "I give unto them eternal life." "Who shall separate us from the love of Christ", or from the Christ who loves us? None. Those whose portion is the Lord are happy with Him and with nothing but Him. This is the genuine witness of all the people of God in every age. "Whom have I in heaven but thee and there is none (or nothing) on earth that I desire besides Thee." When Christ spoke to the woman of Samaria he reminded her–and convinced her too– that no earthly favour would ever satisfy her soul. Only "the Gift of God" which was Christ Himself. He is the Well of Life. He is the Bread of Life. He is the Tree of Life. God gave us Christ, and Christ gave us Himself that He might be our portion for ever. Happy are they who can say:

"God is of mine inheritance
And cup the portion."

"There is none good but God." "O, taste, and see, that the Lord is good." Moses, who was offered all the pleasures, honours and riches of Egypt rejected them when he came to know of "the goodwill of Him who dwelt in the bush". It was he who passed out of time with these words on his lips: "Happy art thou, O Israel who is like unto thee, O people saved by the Lord!" When Solomon sat under the shadow of Christ, the Tree of Life, and tasted of His goodness, all that he possessed of earthly riches became "vanity", or emptiness. When Paul tasted of the love of Christ he counted all other things as "dross". It was he who afterwards wrote the immortal words: "Love envieth not." "I have," as one put it, "Christ, what want I more?" And when we receive Him all things worth having are ours also. "He that spared not His own Son but delivered Him up for us all, how shall He not with Him also freely give us all things."

We know that, in this life, we have but a foretaste of good things to come; but if the earnest is so sweet and precious, what shall it be when we come to the place where we shall "hunger no more, neither thirst any more". "O, how great is Thy goodness which Thou hast laid up for them who fear Thee!" Remember also that in all your afflictions all things are going to *work together for your good.*

Dear friend, you who may be still a stranger to God, there is no escaping the dread alternative to this enjoyment of Him. It is sin and the wages which it pays. For the wages of sin is death—the death that shall never die. How deeply we value our natural life! Bur man's folly is seen in the way he despises and rejects that life which alone can bring to soul and body eternal peace, satisfaction and unspeakable joy.

Just a word now on:

III. The opportune moment —"Acquaint NOW thyself with Him."

It is possible that you may have agreed with everything which I have said on these words. You may give your assent to the truth that no greater blessing could be yours than to have a saving knowledge of God, and that real peace and everlasting good come to men through a personal knowledge and acceptance of Jesus Christ as He is freely offered to us in the Gospel. But lurking in your mind there is a sin which Satan uses to bring many to eternal destruction. Satan of whose presence and wiles you may be unaware may have been whispering in your mind: "Yes, what the preacher says is true. You should think it over, and make your decision by and by. But for this you will, no doubt, be given a more convenient time. There is, of course, another day coming. Meantime there's a lot ot be done. Besides, a sudden breakaway from your usual customs and companions may involve you in much embarrassment. Better far to let well alone for the time being. Certainly later on, but not 'NOW' . . ." And so the well concealed enemy of your soul is gently leading you to the very precipice of eternal woe. It is in the path of *procrastination*—the deceptive thief of time by whom many come to grief. Time is one of God's most precious gifts to lost men. God commands us to redeem it without delay. What have you done with all your past days and years? They have all passed away as a tale that is told, and in the case of many, as a tale that is not worth telling. All that your life—without this acquaintance with God—tells is a story of shame and fearful neglect. We were shapen in iniquity. We were born in sin. We have lived in sin. But how will you die? There are millions in heaven who were born in sin and who lived in sin, but not one who died in sin. But many who died in their sins had hoped, like Balaam of old, that they would have died the death of the righteous and that their last end would be like this. But they did not. Why? They made light of, or ignored, God's word and warning. "Behold NOW is the day of salvation." "Today if ye will hear His voice harden not your heart." "Escape for thy life". "Acquaint thyself NOW with Him." Here, at this moment, you may, like the publican in the temple, bow your head in prayer: "God be merciful to me a sinner." And before he walked out of the temple he was justified and saved by the power and grace of the One who alone can save sinners. "Jesus of Nazareth passeth by." And you beware, my dear friend, lest in your last moments you should, like the foolish virgins, make the dread discovery that finally His door is for ever shut and the day of grace is for ever gone. "Come *now* and let us reason together, saith the Lord, though your ins be as scarlet, they shall be as white as snow, and though they be red like crimson, they shall be as wool. "NOW." "NOW." Is your answer, "Yes" or "No"?

May He bless His own Word. Amen.

LOVE THAT PASSES KNOWLEDGE

"*But we preach Christ crucified.*"–I Cor. Ch. 1, v. 23

Many changes have taken place in our world since these words were first written. But there are two things which remain unchanged. Sin in all its power is still here and, as we know, death is the wages which it pays. And when we speak of death we are not to think merely of natural, or physical death, but of that death which is also spiritual and eternal. Opposite the dread power of sin, however, is the changeless and saving power of the Gospel. As nothing could heal the ailing world of Paul's day but the leaves of the Tree of Life, the only remedy for this so-called "progressive", but sin-sick, age is the everlasting Gospel of Christ crucified.

The days we live in are evil. Our age is laden with peril. Men are, no more holding their breath for fear of these things which are coming upon the earth. The enemy of mankind is come in like a flood. Our moral degeneration and spiritual apostacy may be seen by all whose eyes are open. Our "permissive" society is touching the lowest moral level in the history of our nation. And there can be no salvation, or any alleviation of our danger, apart from the Gospel preached in the power of the Spirit. The only refuge for mankind is Christ and Him crucified. These words, therefore, should be:

I. The theme of a true gospel ministry

While it is our duty to preach Christ in His pre-incarnate and exalted glory, His death on the Cross is the core of the Gospel. While we preach Christ on the Throne reigning as King over all, Christ on the Cross is the only way to God. Not His example but His expiation, not His second coming but His first should be the very centre of our preaching. The hope of the Church with regard to His coming again is laden with comfort. "For unto them that look for Him shall He appear the second time without sin unto salvation." But that hope derives all its consolation and blessing from His finished work of redemption. He entered our world in our nature that He might save us from our sins. It is His first coming that makes His coming again so endearing to His own people.

In the days of Paul there were those both among Jews and Greeks to whom Christ crucified was "a stumbling block" and "foolishness". The correct religious formalist who of his own "good works" was, as he thought, paving a way into God's favour is still with us. So also are "the thinkers" or "philosophers" who by "great swelling words of vanity" complicate the Divine simplicity of the Gospel and who dismiss the death of Christ as irrelevant to man's real needs and problems. There are also many who make the teachings and example of our Lord their theme, but to whom His blood, or death, is an offence and an absurdity. Such men close the only door into Heaven in their own faces. They have no Gospel to preach. God can never be known, approached, or enjoyed but through the death of His Son.

What is it that lends such glory and efficacy to this theme? It is, in a word, the incomparable glory of the person Who thus gave His Life a ransom for many. Who is Christ? To the modernist, or to the false prophets–and there are many such–of this age. He is only a man. They allow that He was in some ways great and unique and in a different dimension to most men, but they deny His Deity or His own claim to be equal with God. Christ, is the Eternal Son of God "by Whom are all things, through Whom are all things" and for Whom. He is "the heir of all things". The uniform witness ofScripture is that Christ is God in the Second Person of the Trinity. "I and the Father are One."

What, in the light of Scripture that we must realise is that He would not accept satisfaction on behalf of sinful men from any person inferior to Himself. And this is exactly how God speaks of Him as, He, voluntarily and in love, came under the stroke of His justice as the Surety and Substitute for sinners. "Awake o sword against My Shepherd and against the man who is my fellow." The word "fellow" her means One who was, and is, His eternal Companion and Equal.

But it was necessary that He Who was to redeem us should be also a man; for God could not, in justice, lay the iniquities of His peopld on One Who was not also a man. It was man who sinned, and it was against God he sinned. Therefore, He who was to die for man's sin must be a man Himself. So Christ was, "and continues to be, God and Man in two distinct natures, and one Person for ever". Herein we see the glorious mystery of the Godhead, God manifest in the flesh. "The Word was made flesh." This truly is a mystery which in its height and depth is beyond the comprehension of men and angels. Christ's human nature was the immediate creation of the Holy Ghost. He did not come by ordinary generation. He took our nature with its infirmities, but without its sin. "That holy thing which shall be born of thee, shall be called the Son of God." These were the words which God's heavenly messenger spoke to the virgin mother.

We also know that sin and Satan are such powers and that only God in the whole range of His Omnipotence could break their sway and destroy their works. The power of sin is such that no fallen creature could ever deliver himself from it apart from the power and help of God. Satan was the strong man armed who kept his goods in peace till a stronger than he invaded his dominions and bruised his head. It was on the Cross, in all seeming weakness, that Christ put away sin by the sacrifice of Himself and forever spoiled principalities and powers.

That "Christ crucified" was God dying in our nature and in our stead may be seen in another way. The burden of imputed sin–the sins of a great multitude which no man can number–was so inconceivably great that only

God could bear it and remove it from our persons forever. It was a burden so heavy that only God in the person of the Father could lift it and place it on His Beloved Son. "Who bore our sins in His own body on the tree." There are some who give the doctrine of imputation a meaning which, we believe, is alien to the witness of Scripture. They say that Christ did not bear our *actual* sins and transgressions. But what say the scriptures? "Surely He hath borne our griefs and carried our sorrows . . . and the Lord hath laid on Him the iniquity of us all." These words are confirmed as the word "surely "surely" or "verily" means "by the very oath of God". They declare that it *was* our actual sins with all the sorrow which they produced that Christ bore on the cross.

Thus we see that it was the Person Who made an atonement Who also rendered that offering so infinitely acceptable to God, and so infinitely efficacious in reconciling us to God. But the emphasis here is not only on the glory of the Person Who died but also on the supreme necessity of proclaiming the implications of His death and the blessings which it procured for lost sinners. "We preach Christ crucified." Let me therefore say a word on:

II. The necessity to proclaim this theme

Paul says elsewhere that necessity was laid upon him to preach this Gospel and that any neglect on his part to do this would expose him to God's rebuke. "Woe unto me if I preach not the Gospel." But Paul was faithful to God, and His Word, and to his own conscience and commission. Nor would he have the blood of souls on his head.

It is necessary to proclaim this truth since God in His Word says only the blood of Christ could open the door of Heaven to sinful men. The high priest of Israel could not enter into the holiest of all on the great Day of Atonement without blood. That great transaction was typical of Christ Who after dying on the Cross entered in "within the veil" with His Own blood. By His death we are reconciled to God and made to draw near to Him. In the temple in Jerusalem there was written on "the middle wall of partition" a warning that no Gentile could go beyond that wall but at the risk of losing his life. But Christ by His death broke it down. All men may come to God at the Throne of Grace through the merits and death of His dear Son. In the words of another when Christ entered Heaven He left the door open behind Him. And it shall so remain till the last of His people join the great multitude who sing night and day the song of Moses and of the Lamb.

We would also state that it is only through Christ crucified that we can have peace with God. He alone is our peace. Where did all the attributes of God rest and rejoice in the salvation of sinners? In the death of Christ. "He shall rest in His love" that love which is revealed in the gift and in the death of His Beloved Son. Here truth and mercy meet and righteousness and peace kiss each other. Here were also find rest. Peace with God reigns through the righteousness of His Son. Nothing can give peace to the awakened conscience of the sinner, but the sprinkling of that blood which speaketh better things than the blood of Abel. It was in anticipation of His vicarious death that Christ uttered these words: "Peace I leave with you, my peace I give unto you . . . Let not your heart be troubled neither let it be afraid." This is the peace that shall flow through the souls of His people like a river forever and ever.

As nothing can bring peace to the conscience but the blood of Christ, there is nothing on the other hand within this vast universe that can cleanse us from *all* sin but His blood. Sin is a defilement of the soul of man. "We are altogether as an unclean thing." It is that which changed our world from being a paradise into a moral and spiritual dunghill, Under the typical dispensation God wearied of that incessant ritual which only touched the surface of this plague. Therefore Christ said, "Sacrifice and offering thou didst not desire. Then said I, Lo I come; in the volume of the book it is written of me." It was not to the Levitical priest or to the blood of bulls and of goats that David went for cleansing, but to another Priest and to another Fountain. His prayer was to the Great High Priest in Heaven, "Purge me with hyssop and I shall be clean; wash me and I shall be whiter than snow." Satan may distress sin-stricken souls by making them fear that their sins are beyond remission; but "the blood of Jesus Christ His Son cleanseth us from all sin". His merits rise infinitely beyond all our ill-deservings.

"The dying thief rejoiced to see
That fountain in his day,
And there may I, though vile as he,
Wash all my sins away."

In Heaven there is an eternal harmony in the song of God's redeemed. Their deliverance and cleansing from the power and defilement of sin are ascribed to Christ and His death on the Cross. "Unto Him Who loved us and *washed* (or loosed) us from our sin in His own blood . . . They washed their robes and made them white in the blood of the Lamb."

Dear friend, have you been to this Fountain opened by God for sin and uncleanness; or are you like Pilate and thousands of other deceived souls, thinking that by washing your hands in the impure water of mere outward reformation your guilt and sin are removed? Beware, my friend, beware. Your dream will end in eternal disaster.

We also preach Christ crucified because the Holy Spirit will not bless or acknowledge any other message or Gospel in the conversion of sinners or in the reviving of the Church of God. This was the theme through which thousands were added to the Church in the Day of Pentecost. It was through the pure preaching of the finished work of Christ, and the utter rejection and exclusion of all the heresies of the papal system, that the Sun of righteousness arose with healing in His wings on Europe at the Reformation. Our Puritan fathers put the supreme emphasis on Christ's Person and Atonement in all their preaching. The same was true of the great evangelical revivals by which our own land was so richly blessed with the spiritual dew of Heaven. God opened the windows of Heaven and poured us out a blessing through which many were brought from death to life. It was when John announced that Christ was the Lamb of God that the Holy Dove–the source of all spiritual power–descended and rested or remained on the person of Our Lord. This anointing did not remain with Himself. It went down to the skirts of His garment. It extended, in other words, to His mystical body the church. It was when the prophet had the sacrifice, or the blood, on the altar that the fire consumed it. This was an event that coincided with the destruction of Baal's prophets and which was also followed by the sound of the abundance of rain. If our Protestant churches were blessed today with a converted ministry who preached the ruin of man, through the Fall, redemption only through Christ's blood, and regeneration through the power of the Holy Spirit, how soon would our deserts blossom as the rose and a new spiritual day-spring from on high visit us. May God raise up many such men among us in this day of small things.

There was one other thing which constrained Paul to preach Christ and Him Crucified. Not only that here we have a manifestation both of God's wisdom and power, but also the greatest revelation that shall ever be given to man of God's love–God's love in giving us His Son, and the Son's love in giving us Himself. Christ gave Himself for us that He might give Himself to us. Is that not a most precious truth?

Nothing has more power over the heart of man than the love that is revealed in the death of Christ. It is here His love touched its greatest depth. This is what enables us to see into the very heart of God. "The Son of God Who loved me and gave Himself for me." A godly minister once said that he could not tell what affected him more–the sight he got of himself as a sinner, or of Christ's love in dying for such a great sinner as he was. It is at the Cross before such love "so amazing, so divine" that we bow our heads remembering that He Who loved us was once the subject of our malice, against Whom we had so grievously sinned. "They shall look on Him Whom they have pierced and mourn." When, in Bunyan's "Pilgrims' Progress", Christiana came in view of the Cross she exclaimed: "It makes my heart bleed to think that He should bleed for me." This love is not something the evidence of which we see in something objective or external to our-selves. It is shed abroad in our heart. He Who gave Himself for us is He Who communicates Himself to our soul and causes us to exclaim with all His people: "O taste and see that God is good." It passes knowledge.

We see His love not only in what He gives but also in what He takes away. Our sins and our iniquities, He remembers no more. They are forever put away "as far as the East is distant from the West".

Now let me say just one word in conclusion on:

III. The universal appropriateness of this proclamation

In the days of Paul the moral and spiritual state of the nations was truly at a low ebb. The huge Roman Empire, with all its co-called "culture" and military power, was a veritable sink of iniquity. In his Epistle to the Romans, and in his sermons at Athens, he touches on how deep the process of degen-eration had become and how unspeakably heinous were the sins which were, without shame, practised in society. On all sides there was an appalling spiritual darkness. Men were groping their way in the dark, and moving toward everlasting destruction. Well he knew that no power on earth could save man, or prevent God's judgment from having its exercise on nations which had sold themselves to do evil. But God had given him a glorious gospel to preach of which he was not ashamed. It alone was the power of God unto salvation to all who would receive its blessings and believe on Him "Who would have all men to be saved".

It is, historically speaking, or in the context of time, a far cry from Paul's day to our own; but are we not, with all our many privileges and blessings, rapidly sinking to the same low level? The moral and spiritual state of our own nation, for example, is terrifying in the extreme. One could go on enumerating such evils as drunkenness, gambling, drug addiction, immorality, sodomy, and all forms of lawlessness and violence till our hearts are almost broken, and these are largely condoned by society. But, O, how we should bless God that the Bible is still in our hand and that the same glorious gospel which Paul preached may still be preached here. Let us value it. Let us proclaim it. It is God's last word to mankind. It is the only door of escape from everlasting destruction. Christ and Him crucified is our only hiding-place from the wind—the only refuge from all the tempests and dangers to which our sin has exposed us. And these are nearer than many of us think. There is no place to hide but in the cleft Rock of Ages. May God give us the will, the wisdom and the grace to flee unto Him to hide us.

THE NIGHTLESS WORLD

"For there shall be no night there."–Rev. Ch. 21, v. 25

In heaven there is neither a natural nor a spiritual night, only a perpetual day. Although we live in a fallen sinful world the silent universe by which we are surrounded imparts a loveliness to it which is beyond words. The sun graces each day, while the moon and the stars grace each night. These declare God's glory and speak of His eternal power and Godhead. The words of our text, however, speak particularly, not of physical darkness, but of that appalling spiritual night which descended upon our world through sin. There is a spiritual darkness in which, left to themselves, all men grope in utter blindness. This darkness had its source in sin. Satan is spoken of in God's Word as the power of darkness. And when by sin Satan invaded the soul of man he made him a child of darkness. This is what the Apostle reminds God's people of in the words: "Ye were sometime darkness, but now are ye light in the Lord"–although only in Heaven shall they be finally separated from sin.

In Heaven:

I. There shall be no night of sin

Although God's people are the children of the day on whose soul the Sun of Righteousness is risen with healing in His wings, only in the world of glory shall their night of sin be forever gone. But who among us can envisage a world or a state of existence where no sin is present? Since we were born in sin, and lived all our days surrounded by sin, with sin within our beings, this is something beyond our comprehension. "It doth not yet appear what we shall be; but we know that when He shall appear we shall be like Him; for we shall see Him as He is."

However great her love of Christ and her nearness to Him in this world here, the Church could not but long for the passing of her night of sin, which so often distressed her. "Until the day break and the shadows flee away, turn, my beloved, and be thou like a roe or a young hart upon the mountains of Bether." All the people of God shall enter that glorious world without sin: for Christ shall present them to Himself "without spot or wrinkle or any such thing." "And there appeared a great wonder in Heaven, a woman clothed with the sun and the moon under her feet, and upon her head a crown of twelve stars." It is from their glorified and exalted Redeemer that all His people shall derive their eternal glory and happiness.

This nightless world demands that all those who inhabit it should have a perfect righteousness, a new nature and an eternal holiness. In other words, all who are there are adorned in Christ as their righteousness: they are born again from above and they are sanctified by God's Spirit who used all their tribulations in this world to that end. In this tabernacle they often groan under the body of sin, but "there is no night of sin there". There shall they behold, with an ever deepening love within their hearts towards Him, the One Who washed them from their sins in His own blood and Who removed them from their beings for ever "as far as east is distant from the west". Not only so, He shall remember them no more. And as there shall be no night of sin in Heaven,

II. There shall be no night of ignorance or defective knowledge there

In this world God's people are enlightened by The Holy Spirit in the knowledge of Christ. They know the Lord. They know whom they have believed. God has opened their eyes so that they apprehend things spiritual and eternal. They see the wonders which are present in His Word, but only in part and dimly as through a glass. There are many aspects of God's Word and Providence the meaning of which remains concealed from our eyes. "It is the glory of God to conceal a thing." And within these two realms we can say with God's Prophet: "Verily Thou art a God that hidest thyself, O God of Israel, the Saviour.".The Lord Jesus reminded us that there are awe-inspiring events related to the future which are known to God only. In speaking, for example, of that great day which shall seal the destiny of all men, He said: "But of that day and hour knoweth no man, no, not the angels of Heaven, but my Father only."

There are many instances in God's Word of those who enjoyed much of God's favour, and to whom He gave great and precious promises but who in the unfolding of His Providence and in the fulfilment of His promises often discovered that His thoughts were not their thoughts; and that as the Heavens are higher than the earth so were His ways higher than their ways. His ways are in the deep and He often "moves in a mysterious way." In relation to His Providence and Grace God speaks to His people but only in eternity shall the darkness which often surrounds them be finally dispelled and their day be perfect. God therefore exhorts them to trust in His name even when they walk in darkness and have no light. Jacob, the man whom God so richly blessed, as he stood surrounded by so many frowning providences, exclaimed, "Against me are all these things." But his end in this world was like a morning without a cloud. The Lord lit his candle and turned his darkness into light. His path, like that of all the people of God, was "as the shining light that shineth more and more unto the perfect day". In the glorious world above their sun shall no more go down neither shall their moon be darkened. "In that day," said our Lord to His disciples, "ye shall ask me nothing." There we shall know even as we are known, for "there is no night there."

And there shall be:

III. No night of sorrow there

How often do we think of God's promises as if they were all laden with consolations; but one of His promises to His people is: "In this world ye shall have tribulation." "These are they that come out of great tribulation", was the answer to the Apostle John's question when he asked one of the glorified beings who stood before the throne who those were clothed in white robes and singing before the throne of God and of the Lamb.

Christ spoke of His Church in her painful environment here as a lily among thorns. They are a people who participate in the sufferings of Christ. "For thy sake we are killed all the day; we are counted as sheep for the slaughter." They were chosen in the furnace of affliction and in that furnace He leaves them till all the sinful dross which clings to their beings is for ever removed. "When He hath tried me," said the suffering Job, "I shall come forth as gold." The waters of Marah were put into the cup of His people from the days of Abel and shall so remain till the last of His loved ones are Home. And among the figures which the Holy Spirit uses in Scripture to describe the sorrows of the true Church in this world is that of a voyage through tempestuous seas and darkness.

"They mount to heaven, then to the depths
they do go down again:
Their soul doth faint and melt away
with trouble and with pain."

When we are passing through such nights we might think, like God's Prophet, that there is no sorrow like our sorrow; but "the same afflictions are accomplished in our brethren who are in the world". "The afflictions of Joseph" are known in some measure to all the children of faith. Their greatest sorrows, needless to say, arise from their conciousness of the evil of sin or the plague of their own heart. While they grieve over the wickedness which prevails in the external world and, sad to say, within the visible church, they, like the doves of the valley, mourn every one for his own iniquity. They come more and more to realise that all their sins are against the God whom they ought to love and are grievous to the blessed and ever-loving Spirit who dwells within their souls. David's confession and plea were: "Against thee, thee only, have I sinned and done this evil in thy sight." "Take not thy Holy Spirit away."

Often, it is when the come under the rod of His chastisement that God's people know their acutest sorrow. And here we have one of the paradoxes of Christian experience. His smitings may be severe. They may touch our bodies and souls to such an extent that we may feel that they are more than they are able to endure. They may also with shamefacedness know the background of the Lord's chastenings. Not only may our hearts be filled with grief, but a sense of guilt may deeply disturb our conscience and its peace. How appropriate to all true believers are God's words with regard to the chastenings and penitence of Ephraim. "I have surely heard Ephraim bemoaning himself thus: 'Thou hast chastened me, and I was chastened, as a bullock unaccustomed to the yoke: turn thou me and I shall be turned, for thou art the Lord my God. Surely after that I was turned I repented: and after that I was instructed I smote upon my thigh: I was ashamed, yea, even confounded, because I did bear the reproach of my youth'." Then in the midst of all his godly sorrow came these endearing words from the lips of Him Whose "mouth is most sweet", Whose love is eternal, and Who pities His children more than a father pities his ailing child: "Is Ephraim my dear son? is he a pleasant child? for since I spoke against him, I do earnestly remember him still: therefore my bowels are troubled for him. I will surely have mercy upon him, saith the Lord."

A suffering and much chastened man one night retired to bed. And as he slept he dreamed. In his dream he saw an elderly and sad-looking man sitting in a room. Then the man who dreamed quoted the words: "Whom the Lord loveth He chasteth and scourgeth every son whom He receiveth." And as he quoted these words he saw the face of the old man radiating with peace and joy. On awakening he realised anew that one of the greatest proofs which the Lord can give His people of His love comes to them through their suffering. Their nights of weeping may be many; but joy cometh in the morning–the morning that shall never be followed by a night, "for there is no night there". "Sorrow and sighing shall flee away."

And:

IV. There shall be no night of fear or temptation in that blessed world

Our greatest fears often come through our temptations. And the temptations of God's people take many forms. Satan's fiery darts are many and of different kinds. He knows that what may be a terror to one may not greatly affect another. And Scripture and Christian biography often reveal that the greatest of God's saints have frequently passed through the darkest nights. Is there any part of Scripture that, for example, mirrors the afflictions of saints more than the Book of Psalms? David was a man after God's own heart and therefore Satan often led him into darkness. "For the enemy hath persecuted my soul: he hath smitten my life down to the ground: he hath made me to dwell in darkness as those that have been long dead. Therefore is my spirit overwhelmed within me: my heart within me is desolate."

How great was Paul's fear when the adversary, with an unknown temptation, buffeted his soul. What his thorn in the flesh, the messenger of Satan, was is not disclosed. Who knows, my tired and tempted friend, but that it might have been what is presently your own trial? Was there ever a man who passed through fears and temptations such as harassed the soul of John Bunyan? He looked upon his sins as unpardonable, and beyond the reach of God's mercy or forgiveness. Satan, as the spirit of blasphemy, invaded his soul over a long period of time. Another God-blessed man, Duncan Matheson, was over a long period of time in the same dark vale. Others could speak of temptations to unbelief, to atheism, to covetousness and other sins which they had to endure and battle against for many days.

It is a remarkable fact that those who have done the most to advance the cause of Christ in the world, and to bring many souls to Christ, have often been the subjects of the greatest temptations. Perhaps Satan knew that such men would inflict more damage upon his own kingdom than others. But none who bears the Lord's image and in whose heart there is love to Him can hope to escape the malice of the wicked one. Our secret spiritual exercises he dreads and opposes, especially when we plead with God to destroy his kingdom and to bruise his head under our feet.

Some of God's people were at times afraid that the evil thoughts which so often distressed them reflected their real selves, and that if they were the subjects of God's saving grace such temptations would not lodge in their hearts. But not until the day dawns shall these fears about which we so often cried to God be finally and wholly dispelled. In our fears one of our greatest comforts is that "the Brother born for adversity" was, although He did no sin and was incapable of sinning, tempted in all points like as we are These words show that to be tempted is in itself no sin. Only when we yield to it do we sin; but when we endure it and by His grace overcome it we are, in the words of the Apostle James, truly blessed. "Blessed is the man that endureth temptation; for when he is tried, he shall receive the crown of life, which the Lord hath promised to them— that love Him." Meantime remember His words: "My grace is sufficient for thee." "They overcame by the blood of The Lamb and by the word of His testimony." In Heaven we shall be eternally beyond the reach of all our fears, for "there is no night there".

Nor shall there be–

V. A Night of spiritual desertion or loneliness there

When we speak of spiritual desertion we must not conclude that the Lord is ever separate from His people. That cannot happen. "I will never leave thee nor forsake thee." He is ever beside us. Within the context of Christian experience, however, there are seasons when God's presence is very real to us. We then say with Jacob at Bethel, "The Lord is in this place", Or with the Church when she said, "My beloved is mine and I am His". Or with Thomas who, when confronted with heart-melting evidences of His unspeakable love, His Deity and resurrection from the dead, exclaimed: "My Lord and my God."

In these seasons of spiritual enjoyment we may say with David: "In my prosperity I said I shall never be moved." Soon, however, clouds descended upon his soul which compelled him to say: "Thou didst hide Thy face and I was troubled." The Church, whose heart was warmed and gladdened by her Lord's love and sweet presence, we now hear weeping and asking the questions: "Saw ye Him whom my soul loveth?" "O! that I knew where I might find Him" was the cry of Job in his day of darkness and pain. Mary Magdalene wept as she asked the question before the empty grave: "They have taken away my Lord, and I know not where they have laid Him." Then a voice reached her ear: "Woman, why weepest thou?" He was there beside her. And just as He said to His disciples when He was about to ascend unto Heaven, "Lo, I am with you alway", He reminded her that while His bodily presence would soon be taken from her He would be nearer to her by His spiritual presence and by His love within her soul after

He had ascended unto His Father and to her Father. If there are times in our lives when clouds take Him out of our sight, let us remember His promise: "And ye now therefore have sorrow: but I will see you again and your heart shall rejoice and your joy no man taketh from you." In the nightless world above they shall see Him as He is, and "His name shall be written in their foreheads". Now we see Him darkly as through a glass, but there face to face. There also in the great congregation shall they enjoy unbroken communion with all the saints of God.

When the Apostle John wrote this Book he was in the isle of Patmos. As far as earthly companions were concerned he was there alone. Many of these who had been his companions in other days had gone to their heavenly rest. Many of God's people in every age had to tread the path of loneliness. They were pilgrims and strangers here. The world knew them not, and they had no desire to have fellowship with a godless world or "with the unfruitful works of darkness". Men like Enoch and Micah walked in the path of loneliness with God only as their companion. David, persecuted by many in the nation, sought refuge in remote solitary places where he was like a "pelican in the wilderness". "Woe is me that I sojourn in Mesech, that I dwell in the tents of Kedar." It was because of his devotion to God, to his Word and to the testimony of Jesus Christ that John was banished to this lonely isle. He speaks of himself as companion to all who suffer tribulation for Christ.

But whatever our circumstances or our place of abode here a sense of loneliness may often touch our lives. Do we not feel lonely when one by one of our friends in the Lord are taken away? Once I was present at the funeral of an excellent man of God. An elderly minister who had been his friend on earth engaged in prayer. "Lord," he said, "some of Thy people whom we knew in this world are now with Thyself in glory, and we long to be with them."

But is it not true that our days of so-called loneliness are often our happiest days? We become conscious that The Lord is with us. His gracious presence becomes real to us. We would rather then be alone lest our peace should be distrubed by the presence and conversation of those who may be strangers to Him, and ignorant of the exercises and ejoyment of God's flock. The Church, in the enjoyment of Christ's presence, pleaded with the daughters of Jerusalem–those whose religion was merely formal–not to disturb her Beloved as long as He was pleased to stay with her.

There is one night the approach of which we may often fear. The way to our eternal rest lies through the unknown valley of the shadow of death; but have we not heard of many of God's people who were happier in this vale than ever they were on their pilgrimage journey? They could say with David: "I shall fear no evil for Thou art with me." A timid girl in one of our Hebridean isles was asked by her father to visit a place at the end of a long and lonely road. "It may be dark," he said, "before you get home, but don't you be afraid for I shall meet you in the way myself." When in due course he went forth to meet her she was quite near her home. "Well, my dear," remarked her father, "were you not afraid coming home along in the darkness?" Her answer was: "No, for I knew that you would meet me in the way as you promised."

Who is going to accompany us as we cross the last river, and as we enter the vale of death? Who, but The Beloved of our soul– The One Who conquered death and Who gave us His promise: "When thou passest through the waters I shall be with you." A few years ago a dear friend of mine went on a visit to the Holy Land. One day when he was passing over the River Jordan in a conveyance he remarked to a friend how good it would be if their passage out of this world would be as pleasant and as easy as their literal crossing of that river. Then there was silence. He bowed his head, and breathed his last breath in this world of time. His soul was forever with The Lord. "This God is our God for ever and ever: He shall be our guide even unto death"–till we reach that happy country where our sun shall no more go down "for there is no night there".

Blessed and happy day for all those who have the oil of grace in their vessels! Amen.

LEANING ON THE BELOVED

"*Who is this that cometh up from the wilderness leaning upon her beloved*?"–Songs, Ch. 8, v. 5

These words are before us in the form of a question, and as we meditate on them there are several relevant questions which we might ask, and which, by the help of the Spirit, we would endeavour to answer. The first question is:

I. Who is this person?

This glorious Song, or allegory, speaks, we know, of Christ and the Church, and the Church is the one that is here spoken of. There are many definitions and explanations given in these times, as to what, or who, the true Church of God is, and how it may be identified in this world. We know that in the ultimate sense the Church is made up of those whom God loved, and who were chosen in Christ from all eternity. These are they for whom Christ died, and whom He shall present to Himself at last "without spot or wrinkle or any such thing". These are all embraced in God's eternal covenant of grace. "Whom he did foreknow He also did predestinate, whom he did predestinate, them He also called and whom he called them he also justified, and whom he justified them he also glorified." These people are all known to God, and to no one else. "The foundation of God standeth sure, having this seal, the Lord knoweth them that are His."

But how can we identify the Church in this world? Well, she answers to the description which God gives of her in His Word. The Church is made up of a people whom God has changed and renewed by the Holy Spirit. "The church of the first born" is defined as those who are born again. They are all vessels unto honour. And they are not empty vessels. The love of Christ is shed abroad in their heart by that same Spirit who quickened them in a day of His power. Their love, in the deepest sense, rests on God Himself. They also love His Word, His people, and His house–the place "where His honour dwelleth". In their conduct and worship they seek to adhere to His will as it is revealed in His own Word. They seek to preserve and proclaim "the faith once delivered to the Saints". Those who abide not by His law and testimony have no light in them, and are therefore not His people.

Christ described His people in such a way that they may be known even to a godless world. "Ye are the light of the world." "So let your light shine before men." "A city that is set on an hill cannot be hid." They are "epistles of Christ which may be known and read of all men".

This love to God, His Word and His people, is what imparts true unity to the Church of God. "By this shall all men know that ye are my disciples if ye love one another." She is not, in this world, a perfect Church, and there are many minor issues on which her members may differ. Their unity is not something external, or a mere conformity to the rites and traditions of men. It is the fruit of the Spirit, and something for which they pray as our Lord Himself prayed. "I pray that they may be one even as we are one."

We live in a day when graceless men, and swarms of false prophets, are striving hard to bring about a false unity under the name of a world church. Such an ecclesiastical apparatus would include the papal system, which through the past ages, has done all in its power to destroy the true Church of God. This Church would also include all those other churches whose negative, modernistic theology has left them stark naked and lifeless. A fundamental aim of this false ecumenical movement is to "swallow up", or absorb, the true Prophetic, Apostolic and Reformed church, and to silence her voice. But God is within her palaces for a refuge, and He is ever by her side. All her enemies He will bring low. Though she may now be "a very small remnant" her future power and glory are going to be inconceivably wonderful. "Who is she that looketh forth as the morning fair as the moon, clear as the sun and terrible as an army with banners?" Who, but the Church of God blessed and uplifted by her Lord on Whom she ever leans and from Whom all her glory is derived.

Since the Church, in these words, is spoken of as on a journey, let us consider the next question:

II. Where did she come from?

She was not always where she is now. Literally speaking, Israel, among whom the Church of God in the world had its beginning were a people who had a remarkable history behind them. In Egypt, for example, they were in a land of darkness and bondage. They were under sentence of death, and confined to a vast prison. They were, without God's intervention, helpless and without hope. But God saw their affliction and heard their cry. By an outstretched arm and by the blood of His covenant He opened a way for them out of their bondage.

This event was typical of a deeper bondage and a greater salvation. We were all the children of wrath even as others. We were, spiritually speaking, in the land of darkness. We were in the far country of spiritual alienation. We were under the curse of God's holy law, and out of the hands of His justice we could never redeem ourselves. Eternal death was the just and deserved wages of our sin. But in that spiritual grave and helpless state, God, Who convinced us of our lost estate, heard our cry. He passed by us in mercy, and said, "Live". He made our time a time of love. We then saw that it was through the righteousness, merits, and death of His dear Son—the Lamb of God Who in His own Sovereign purpose was slain before the foundation of the world—that God exercised His power and mercy in our salvation. It was through His shed blood that our sins were covered and, like the Egyptian hosts, were cast into the sea of His forgiveness and oblivion. They shall be remembered no more. He drew us with the cords of his love and with the bands of a man. That was the time when we breathed for the first time the sweet air of heaven and tasted of God's love. We came to know something of the glorious liberty of the children of God. It was the day when a new song was born in our hearts. We could say then "Who is a God like unto Thee that pardoneth iniquity and passeth by the transgression of the remnant of his heritage? He retaineth not his anger for ever, because he delighteth in mercy." "O Lord I will praise thee: though thou was angry with me, their anger is turned away and Thou comfortest me."

How lovely is that song which Moses, Miriam and the Children of Israel sang in the day when God redeemed them, led them through the deep, and released them from their enemies. "I will sing unto the Lord for He hath triumphed gloriously . . . The Lord is my strength and my song, and He is become my salvation, He is my God, and I will prepare Him an habitation, my father's God and I will exalt him . . . Thy right hand, O Lord, is become glorious in power . . . The Lord shall reign for ever and ever." "Happy art thou O Israel, Who is like unto thee, O people saved by the Lord." Do you also, dear friend, not remember the hour when the Lord put a new song in your mouth and when He set your feet on the Rock of Ages, and for evermore established your goings in the paths of righteousness? Happy Day! You are no longer in the land of the dead but in the land of the living.

The next question that confronts us is:

III. Where did her Lord bring her?

He led her into the wilderness. The Lord did not bring His people to the land of Canaan immediately after He redeemed them. Their day of joy and their time of love were comparatively brief, although the memory of it was sweet beyond words to all who were Israelites indeed. Soon they came to Marah the waters of which were so bitter that they could not drink them. This trying experience was, we think, symbolic of the many afflictions which they were afterwards to endure in "a great and terrible wilderness", where their souls were often discouraged because of the way. Because of their murmurings and unbelief, they often came under the rod of God's chastisement. "They wandered in the wilderness in a solitary way; they found no city to dwell in. Hungry and thirsty their soul fainted in them." And many were their enemies. Mighty kings and many nations sought their destruction and tried to prevent their possession of "the land flowing with milk and honey".

The significance of these things is clear to the people of God in all ages since then. God does not bring His people to their heavenly rest in the day when they pass from death to life. Some, indeed, are taken to their eternal home within hours or days after they are born into this world, or reborn in God's spirit. It is so with the elect child. It was so with the thief on the cross. But it is one of God's laws within the kingdom of grace that his people should be left here for "a little white". In His prayer of intercession our Lord said: "I pray not that thou shouldest take them out of the world, but that thou shouldest keep them from the evil." Not from trials and afflictions, but "from the evil". It is in this world that the Church passes through the process of sanctification. He Who has His fire in Zion and His furnace in Jerusalem uses all their wilderness afflictions towards this end. The spiritual soil, so to speak, which is being prepared for heaven and in which the plant of grace thrives, must be both ploughed and harrowed. In this way the thorns and briars of our sinful nature are eradicated and destroyed. "Instead of the thorn shall come up the fir tree and instead of the briar shall come up the myrtle tree, and it shall be to the Lord for a name, for an everlasting sign that shall not be cut off." Our spiritual purification necessarily involves pain. As the Psalmist tells us, it is through "fire and the water" that we are at last brought to the wealthy place.

God allows these afflictions that we might know something of the power from which He delivered us. He permits that we sometimes come into depths of trial that we might know how great was our spiritual plight, the power and malice of Satan, the evil of sin, and the enmity of a world which lies in the wicked one. In the one hundred and seventh Psalm we have a picture of the Church of God passing through a great wilderness, through great storms, and other trials. But her end was peace. Her knowledge and appreciation of God's mercy in rescuing her out of her many perils in this life, will deepen her love for Him through eternal ages.

Our Lord Himself was brought into the wilderness, where, for forty days, He was tempted of the devil. No man or angel shall be able to know the depths through which He passed then. "He was tempted in all points like as we are, yet without sin." Though the Prince of this world could find nothing in Him, and although He was incapable of sinning, yet the flood of blasphemy which Satan let loose upon Him brought Him more agony of soul than mere sinful creatures shall ever know.

And yet it is with Him and in Him that His people suffer. "Unto you it is given on behalf of Christ not only to believe in Him, but also to suffer for His sake." They are partakers of His sufferings; and this is one of the greatest privileges that can be conferred upon us in this life.

The Lord also leaves His church in the wilderness of this world to witness for Him. "Ye are my witnesses, saith the Lord." Our witness is necessarily associated with sufferings. When Paul was called to witness for Christ, He said to Annanias: "He is a chosen vessel unto me to bear my name before the Gentiles and kings, and the Children of Israel: for I will show him how great things He must suffer for my sake."

Although the hope of Heaven is unspeakably precious to the Church of God, or to the individual believer, we would tarry here for a while, so that before the night comes, we might do something for the One Who did so much for us. David in his old age, and with a full assurance of God's love and of a happy eternity with God in his soul, prayed that the Lord might still leave him here till he had shown His strength to his own generation and his power to those who were yet to come. There is a great harvest to be reaped. "The harvest truly is plenteous but the labourers are few; pray ye therefore the Lord of the harvest that He might send forth labourers unto His own harvest." "pray ye therefore." We believe that this is the greatest service we can render to God in this our own day. "Arise O Lord, and plead the cause that is thine own." In this Song, the Church is spoken of as "coming out of the wilderness like pillars of smoke". Her prayers, like incense, were for Christ and His Cause, ascending to God night and day. "Prayer shall be made for Him continually." "Men ought always to pray and not to faint."

And what was:

IV. Her exercise of soul in the wilderness

She was "leaning on her Beloved". The word "leaning" signifies her constant dependence on her Lord for the needed daily strength. The wilderness was a place of destitution, but Christ was never a wilderness to His people. In the prophecy of Hosea He speaks of His loving kindness toward His Church. "I will allure her and bring her into the wilderness, and speak comfortably unto her, and I will give her vineyards from thence, and the valley of Achor for a door of hope." He was the Rock which followed her all the way, and from Whom flowed living water. He was the heavenly and hidden manna who nourished her soul day by day. "I am the Bread of Life." "My God shall supply all your needs according to his riches in Glory by Christ Jesus." All that we need in time and throughout eternity dwells in Him. "All my well-springs are in thee." By faith and prayer we come to Him for the needed blessings. "Evermore give us this bread." He reminds us that the journey is great, and commands us, as in the case of the prophet, to arise and eat. And those who wait upon Him have the promise: "They go from strength to strength; everyone of them in Zion appeareth before God."

Her conscious weakness also compels her to lean on her Lord. The Church is the weaker vessel. Many are the burdens that she has to bear in this life. Many are her discouragements in the way. "All these things are against me." Many are the "Hill Difficulties" which she must ascend on the way Home. But He on Whom she leans is an almighty Friend. His grace is ever sufficient for her, and His strength is made perfect in her weakness. "When I am weak then am I strong." Her prayer always is:

"Hold up my goings, Lord, me guide
in those thy paths divine,
So that my footsteps may not slide
Out of those ways of thine."

And no enemy shall ever pluck her out of His hand. Each day she can say, "Hitherto hath the Lord helped us." "This God is our God for ever and ever. He will be our guide even unto death."

Is it not true that we are never nearer our loved ones than when, in need of their help we lean on their arm? And our seasons of peculiar or greater nearness to our Lord often came in our day of weakness, of adversity, of some personal crises, or when, kneeling before Him in prayer, we were given an awareness that He is ever beside us. "Because," said

Asaph, "He is at my right hand I shall never be moved." At such times we may hear that much loved voice whispering gently within our hearts: "Fear not for I am with thee; be not dismayed for I am thy God. Yea, I will help thee; Yea I will strengthen thee; Yea I will uphold thee with the right hand of my righteousness."

But what is it, in the deepest sense, that brought them so near to one another? Was it not their love to one another? It was love, eternal, sovereign, holy and unchangeable that brought Him to her side. Throughout the years of Israel's pilgrimage, He was in their midst. His Glory and Presence were in the Most Holy Place. Night and day the pillar of fire and of cloud was spread over them. There He rested in His love. "The beloved of the Lord"– as the blessing of Benjamin is spoken of–"shall dwell in safety by Him." This is love from which His people can never be separated and which the floods cannot drown.

It was with the cords of love that He drew His Church to His side. And her love to Him, whatever its ebbs and flows in this life, shall never die. "We love Him Who first loved us." It was Samuel Rutherford who once remarked that he was sailing to heaven in the ship of promise and that he longed for the day when it would sink for ever in the ocean of His love.

The last question we ask is:

V. What is her final destination?

She is on the way to a better country, to that city which has foundations and whose Builder and Maker is God. Heaven is the land of her desire. Her treasure is above, and her affections are set on things which are as yet unseen. Christ, with Whom she walked here by faith is all her desire, and to enjoy Him for ever will be the source of her never ending bliss. Here a cry is often in her heart: "Saw ye Him Whom my soul loveth?", but there her sun shall no more go down. "They shall see His face, and His name shall be in their foreheads." There also she shall enjoy the rest which remaineth for the people of God. In her happy Home she shall hunger no more, neither thirst any more. The days of her mourning shall cease, and in eternal communion with her Lord and His people, and singing for ever the praises of Him Who loved her, her joy shall be full.

Let me, in conclusion, quote words from an old German hymn which are expressive of the mutual joy which shall for ever dwell in the heart of Christ and His Bride when in the eternal home they shall meet to part no more.

"Midst the light, and peace and glory
Of the Father's Home;
Christ for me is watching, waiting,
Waiting till I come.

There, amidst the love and glory
He is waiting yet;
On His hands a name is graven
He can ne'er forget.

There amidst the songs of heaven,
Sweeter to His ear,
Is the footfall through the desert,
Ever drawing near.

He and I in that bright glory
One deep joy to share–
Mine, to be for ever with Him,
His, that I am there."

My dear friend, will you be one of His in that day when He shall make up His Jewels? May He bless His Word.

GOD'S GREAT FEAST AND THE WELCOME GUESTS

"*And in this mountain shall the Lord of hosts make unto all people a feast of fat things, a feast of wines on the lees, of fat things full of marrow, of wines on the lees well refined.*"–Isaiah, Ch. 25, v. 6

These words, we believe, are historically related to the restoration of Israel from Babylon where they had been so long in captivity. Their return to Mount Zion, their spiritual pastureland, marked one of the happiest events in their history. God, in answer to their prayers, had restored them to liberty and to the spiritual privileges which they had forfeited through their sins. They were now provided with many tokens of God's favour. But the words must be given a wider, a richer, and a more universal application than what they have in their historical context. They speak of the Gospel feast prepared by God for destitute sinners who are willing to avail themselves of the spiritual and permanent blessings offered to them in Christ. Let us, to begin with, consider:

I. The great provider of this feast–"The lord of Hosts"

In olden times, and especially in the Oriental world, kings and princes, in order to manifest their riches, dignity and kindness, would provide feasts–not always or often for the poor, but for the more honourable of their subjects. And, on an infinitely higher level, the Gospel is a revelation of the kindness of God toward a lost and needy world. Spiritually speaking, all men are on the same level of utter spiritual destitution.

The blessings of this feast shall continue to unfold themselves throughout the ages to come–"That in the ages to come He might show the exceeding riches of His grace in His kindness toward us through Christ Jesus." In the same Epistle to the Ephesians Paul speaks of the sense of indebtedness and eternal thankfulness within the souls of all who come to know the wonderful grace of God. "Blessed be the God and Father of our Lord Jesus Christ who hath blessed us with all spiritual blessings in heavenly places in Christ."

Those great feasts to which earthly kings invited their favoured guests were not prepared after their arrival at their palaces. No: all things were ready and prepared before they entered their banqueting halls. The servants would have spent many hours, if not days, preparing for such great events. The guests would just walk in and sit down to enjoy the varied and rich fare set before them, while the king would welcome them with kindly words and smiles.

And when did God begin to prepare this feast for those who will sit with Him at His table in the glorious and heavenly palace above? All was prepared by Him "before the foundation of the world". Did He not set His table and prepare His banquet within that everlasting Covenant which is "ordered in all things and sure"? Abel, the first of His saints to enter Heaven, would have been welcomed with the same loving and endearing words as all who shall enter it to the end of time. "Come, ye blessed of my Father, inherit the kingdom prepared for you before the foundation of the world." Our Lord comforted His disciples in this world by assuring them that His table in the heavenly kingdom was already prepared for them, and that there, their souls would enjoy for ever the blessings which He by His death had purchased for them. "Ye are they who have continued with Me in My temptations. And I appoint unto you a kingdom, as My Father hath appointed unto Me; that ye may eat and drink at My table in My kingdom."

And *it is in Christ, the Mediator of the new Covenant, that all the blessings of this feast are reserved.* As an Infinite Person He has in Himself an infinite fulness which He shall continue to communicate to His people for ever. "It pleased the Father that in Him fulness should all dwell." In the typical words of Jacob, the blessing rests "on the head of Joseph, and on the crown of the head of Him who was separated from His brethren." David testified that it was in God alone that all his salvation and glory resided–his salvation on earth and his glory in the world to come.

"In God my glory placed is,
and my salvation sure." (Ps. 62.)

This is also a feast that was purchased for us at a great cost. Although all its blessings are bestowed upon us "without money and without price" much did it cost Christ to set and furnish our table with such abundant blessings. All the riches within the universe could not procure the least of these. It was by His humiliation, sorrows and death that He procured these for His people. "Ye know the grace of our Lord Jesus Christ, that, though He was rich, yet for your sakes He became poor, that ye through His poverty might be rich." It was through the shedding of His precious blood that He opened a way of access for us into God's presence and purchased all the goodness reserved for us in Heaven. Even we ourselves are "bought with a price", "with the precious blood of Christ as of a lamb without blemish and without spot". We had sold ourselves for nought. We were debtors to God's Law and Justice to such an extent that we could never meet their claims. Only He could. When the poor prodigal, regenerated and reconciled to God, sat at his father's table he spoke of him as one who was dead but who was alive again. O, the infinite wonder of God's grace that He should in His Beloved Son "freely give us all things!" "O, how great is Thy goodness which Thou hast laid up for them that fear Thee; which Thou hast wrought for them that trust in Thee before the sons of men!"

And think, dear friends, of *the great number who are to participate in this feast.* It is beyond the power of men or angels to know them or to number them. Only the Lord knows those who are His. Only He who counts the number of the stars knows those who make up the great multitude whom He shall present to Himself on the Great Day. Christ shall see of the travail of His soul in the salvation of all His people. He shall be satisfied in the day when the great harvest of His redeemed people shall be gathered into His kingdom.

And it shall be *a feast of eternal duration.* It begins here, but it shall have no end. When the wayward son returned to his father's house and table he saw that there was bread enough and to spare, and he knew that there he would remain all his days. In this life God's people enjoy many harvests, or foretastes of His goodness; but not till they reach the table above shall "they hunger no more, neither thirst any more". God Himself, and nothing else, shall be the cup of their portion. They shall, in perfect love and holiness, enjoy Him for ever. Never shall they hear the words: "Arise, let us go hence." "The Lamb who is in the midst of the throne shall feed them, and shall lead them unto living fountains of waters: and God shall wipe away all tears from their eyes." "We shall be satisfied with the goodness of Thy house, even of Thy holy temple." In this world the bitter herbs of affliction and the waters of Marah are often in their cup, but in the heavenly Canaan these shall be for ever removed. Only His own love and presence shall fill their hearts, and that blessing which He procured –"life that shall never end". And so, dear friends, the Provider of this feast is the God who is love and the God of all grace.

But let me now say a word on:

II. The feast provided

Since God is the Provider of this feast no other feast can compare with it. It is a feast prepared, primarily, for the souls of men. When men prepare feasts, their provisions only satisfy the bodily needs of their guests, and that only for a few hours. There is nothing in this lower world that can satisfy our souls. Man is a spiritual being, and he cannot therefore "live on bread alone, but on every word that proceedeth out of the mouth of God". How sad it is to know that although the blessings of this feast are infinitely more precious, more satisfying, and although they are free and are to endure for ever, only a small remnant of the human race have any interest in them or seek them. Millions, on the other hand, deny that man has a soul and that there is a spiritual, supernatural world. They maintain that only material things have any real existence. To them God's spiritual feast is but a mere dream divorced from reality. But those who have, by a spiritual rebirth, entered God's Kingdom, and who have "tasted that the Lord is gracious", know that to possess the blessings of this feast is the source of everlasting joy. It is something more solid and much nearer to reality than anything pertaining to this life of mere shadows. It is also something outwith the reach and knowledge of all who know not the Lord. "Eye hath not seen, nor ear heard, neither have entered into the heart of man the things which God hath prepared for them that love Him." "This is life eternal to know Thee, the only true God and Jesus Christ whom Thou hast sent."

Certain figures are used in this verse, and in other parts of Scripture, to describe this feast, and these are all very meaningful.

Scripture speaks, for example, of our spiritual infancy and the nourishment provided for us then. The normally healthy child is born with an instinctive desire for what nature has provided for it, and which only its mother can give it. And God's children participate in this feast the day they pass from death to life. "As new born babes they desire the sincere milk of the Word", and by this milk they grow in grace and in the knowledge of their Lord. They are born, not of blood, nor of the will of the flesh, nor of the will of man, but of God." Those who are born of God live by faith on Christ, Who alone is their life. The life of Heaven is within their souls while they are still on earth. Milk and honey were the choice and promised blessings of Canaan, and the Church in the Song is spoken of as having milk and honey under her tongue while she was still on her pilgrimage journey and passing through the wilderness. This feast Christ bestows on His people through His Word. He alone has the words of eternal life. "I have found Thy words and I did eat them up and Thy word was to me the joy and rejoicing of my heart." "How sweet are Thy words unto my taste." With His milk and honey the Lord provides them with the hidden manna; for He is also the bread of life and the tree of life of whose fruits they participate and under whose shadow they dwell. The earnest of the Spirit, or the foretastes they enjoy here of the pleasures which are for evermore at God's right hand, are precious beyond words. In the words of our Catechism, they enjoy " an assurance of God's love, peace of conscience, joy in the Holy Ghost, increase of grace and perseverance therein to the end". The brook of Eschol, or the brook of God's promises, brings many a token for good to all who, in the way of faith, are going from strength to strength to the heavenly Caanan.

Our text speaks of "a feast of fat things full of marrow". These words proclaim that this feast is both rich and nourishing. To all who know this life a song of thanksgiving is born intheir hearts.

"Even as with marrow and with fat
My soul shall filled be;
Then shall my mouth with joyful lips
Sing praises unto Thee."

"We shall be satisfied with the goodness of Thy house, even of Thy holy temple." "Who satisfieth thy mouth with good things; so that thy youth is renewed like the eagle's. On the solemn night of the passover in Israel, the lamb was slain. Its blood was sprinkled on the door posts, and, to sustain God's Israel in the way, they ate its flesh. And this was a typical event. It is through the death of the Lamb of God that we are not only reconciled to God but have access to His life. By faith, and conscious of need, we participate in all the blessings which His death purchased for us. And, figuratively speaking, the sweetest dish on His table will be unbroken communion with Himself.

The next figure used in our text—"wine on the lees well refined"—speaks of the love of Christ, which is "better than wine." All who have tasted of this love know that it passes knowledge. There are no words in our earthly vocabulary that can describe its sweetness. It is a love which is shed abroad in the hearts of all who know the Lord. David with all his poetic gifts, and even when he was inspired by the Spirit of God, could only stand amazed at the unspeakable gift of God's love. "O taste and see that God is good." We can only know it through our personal enjoyment of it. Therefore he appealed to men to taste it for themselves. "Whom having not seen, ye love; in Whom, though now ye see Him not, yet believing, ye rejoice with joy unspeakable and full of glory." No man ever sat at God's feast, and tasted of this love, who desired anything else. And none ever shall. Millions of the human race have said an everlasting farewell to all the pleasures of sin, and to the deceptive enjoyments of this world; but none who tasted of God's goodness shall ever desire any other blessing for their souls. Those who enjoy this love envy nothing which a godless world desires or pursues. "This is all my salvation and all my desire" was David's death-bed confession.

The word *lees* in this verse conveys the idea that this is old wine. This, in fact, is one translation of the word—"old wine well refined". And how old is this love? It was in the heart of God from everlasting. "God is love." "I have loved thee with an everlasting love." How ravishing are those seasons in our life when we can say with the Church, "He brought me to the banqueting house (or the house of wine) and His banner over me was love". And, O, how warming and reviving a drop of this love can be in those seasons when our hearts are cold and when we are weary in the way!

And it is a wine "well refined". Throughout Eternity this pure and holy love shall flow toward us through the merits of Christ. This is what shall impart unutterable sweetness to it. It was on the Cross of Calvary, in agonies unknown, that this love reached its highest level. It is here we come to know what amazing love was in the heart of God toward His people. May the prayer of David be for ever in our hearts.

"Remember me, Lord, with that love
Which Thou to thine dost bear:
With thy salvation, O my God
To visit me draw near."

But not till we appear before Him in the world of glory shall we fully know what His love has procured for us.

Our text also speaks of:

III. The people for whom this feast is provided

It is made "unto all people". To those who know the voice of God in His word there is nothing more obvious or more impressive than His free and universal offer of salvation to all who are willing to avail themselves of His goodness. Christ's last command to His chosen apostles were to go "into all the world and preach the Gospel to every creature." The Bible ends on the same note. "And the Spirit and the bride say, Come. And let him that heareth say, Come. And let him that is athirst come. And whosoever will, let him take the water of life freely." God's invitations to His feast are to all men. "Look unto Me, and be ye saved, all the ends of the earth: for I am God, and beside Me there is no Saviour." His door is open. "All things are now ready." "Compel them to come in that My house may be filled." "Ho, every one that thirsteth, come ye to the waters, and he that hath no money; come ye, buy, and eat; yea, come buy wine and milk without money and without price." "If any man hear My voice," said Christ, "and open the door, I will come in to him, and will sup with him, and he with Me." How tender also are the words of God's wisdom in the Book of Proverbs. "Come, eat of my bread, and drink of the wine which I have mingled. Forsake the foolish, and live; and go in the way of understanding." Elsewhere we hear the appealing voice of our Lord uttering these words: "Wherefore do ye spend money for that which is not bread and your labour for that which satisfieth not? Hearken diligently unto Me, and eat ye that which is good, and let your soul delight itself in fatness." And so, dear friends, I could go on repeating similar phrases from the compassionate and kindly lips of our Lord for the remainder of the day—all addressed to poor needy and sinful men.

This is a doctrine which we should leave unqualified and untouched, just as it emerges from the merciful heart of Him of Whom it is said: "This man receiveth sinners; He eateth and drinketh with them." We must not put stumbling blocks before the blind, but show them the way to Christ and the freeness of His salvation. And all who obey His voice shall sit as His guests at His table for ever. It was Samuel Rutherford who said: "I shall go to the door of Christ, and if I perish I shall perish at His door; but if I perish there I shall perish where no sinner ever perished." With John Bunyan he could say, "Come and welcome to Jesus Christ". Yes; let me repeat: His door is open, His table is furnished, and all the angels of heaven will rejoice if you come and sit there with the great multitude who shall enjoy His feast for ever.

Let me say one last word on:

IV. The place where this feast is provided—"In this Mountain"

In the Bible we find that certain mountains are associated with great events. It was from Mount Sinai that God delivered to mankind His Holy Law which all men are commanded to obey to the end of time. Mount Zion, which is spoken of in one of the Psalms, as the Joy of the whole earth, is typical of the true Church of God which is the dwellingplace of the Most High in this world. The mountain referred to in this verse is what we might call "the Gospel mountain." The Gospel, and the preaching of it, is the highest favour that men can enjoy in this world. It brings us as high as Heaven. It is glad tidings of great joy. It is, in the words of Solomon, "good news from a far country", Christ enetered our world with good tidings to the poor. "The Spirit of the Lord is upon me, because He hath anointed Me to preach the gospel to the poor; He hath sent Me to heal the broken-hearted, to preach deliverance to the captives, and recovering of sight to the blind, to set at liberty them that are bruised, to preach the acceptable year of the Lord." In these blessed words we have a fulfilment of the prophecy: "How beautiful upon the mountains are the feet of Him that bringeth good tidings, that publisheth peace; that bringeth good tidings of good, that publisheth salvation; that saith unto Zion, Thy God reigneth!" In these words of our Lord we have other blessings enumerated than those mentioned in our text. There is the blessing of perfect and everlasting health and salvation. There is the blessing of perfect freedom from the bondage of sin and the dominion of Satan. There is the blessing of spiritual vision–we see the things which are unseen and eternal. There is the blessing of unending peace. These all belong to His guests. Nothing is lacking which is calculated to impart eternal happiness to them all. "Happy art thou, O Israel: who is like unto thee, O people saved by the Lord." But the half has not been told us.

The wonderful thing is that this mountain is not remote from any one of us. It is "this mountain". It is something near and accessible. In other words the blessings of this feast are within our reach. Christ is near to all who call upon Him. We have, for example, the Bible in our hand. We may breathe out our prayer at the throne of grace at any time, and in any place. The Gospel also may be preached within easy reach of our homes. "The word is night thee, even in thy mouth, and in thy heart: that is, the word of faith, which we preach; that if thou shalt confess with thy mouth the Lord Jesus, and shalt believe in thine heart that God hath raised him from the dead, thou shalt be saved." "Draw nigh to God, and he will draw night to you." Here and now. In the overtures of His mercy, in all His gracious invitations, and in this place where we worship, He is passing by. "Jesus of Nazareth passeth by." O beware, my dear friend, lest, by your neglect, you should let God's goodness pass by you for ever. Then nothing awaits you but an eternity of regret and remorse. O, that you were wise and that you would consider your latter end. And if you come to Him just as you are and embrace Him as your Saviour an eternity of joy shall be yours. Then you shall one day be among those of whom it is said:

"They shall be brought with gladness great,
And mirth on every side,
Into the palace of the King,
And there they shall abide."

THE SUFFERING OF GRACE

"And he said unto me, my grace is sufficient for thee; for my strength is made perfect in weakness"–II Cor. Ch. 12, v. 9

Pride, we believe, is the most destructive sin that ever invaded the beings of men and angels. By this sin those angels "who kept not their first estate" were cast for ever into outer darkness. This also is the sin which brought mankind into a state of sin and misery. Satan, who would be a god himself, came to men with this same ugly lie and temptation as that which destroyed himself. "Ye shall be as gods knowing good and evil." And when Adam, who was the federal head of mankind, hearkened to Satan's voice he involved himself and all mere men in self-destruction. This truly is the sin which is at the root of all our woes both in time and in eternity. But how thankful we should be that, unlike fallen angels, God in His sovereign mercy has provided in His Well-Beloved Son a way of escape and a way of redemption for all who believe in His name.

A permanent characteristic of all those whom God saves, is that, like their Lord and Master, they would be clothed with humility. They know that their Lord gives grace to the humble, but that the proud or self-righteous man he knows afar off. Nowhere is the manifestation of pride more unbecoming and more offensive than in the life and behaviour of men and women who profess to know the Lord.

In the church at Corinth there were some who boasted of their spiritual attainments, their works, and of their nearness to God. They even looked upon Paul–one of the brightest spiritual stars who ever graced the Church of God in this world–as inferior to themselves. They believed that he was not given such views of the glory and reality of eternal and spiritual things such as they enjoyed. It was in order to correct this estimate of his spiritual life that he wrote this chapter. For a moment he lifts the curtain that they might see how awe-inspiring some of his Christian experiences were. This he did under compulsion. "Ye have compelled me." But Paul did not glory in these "visions and revelations of the Lord". There were only three things in which he gloried. He gloried in his Lord, by whose grace alone he was what he was. He gloried in his Cross, and he gloried in his own infirmity. We see how great his humility was in the way in which he speaks of himself in the third person, as if he was speaking of someone else. "I knew a man in Christ." In these words he also gives us a perfect definition of a true Christian, he is a "man in Christ". A Christian is a regenerated man united to Christ by faith, and deriving all his life, his strength and all his spiritual blessings from Christ alone. He is a man who has nothing and is nothing in himself, but to whom Christ "is all and in all".

For a brief while I should like to dwell on three things related to Paul's experience given in this chapter. We have to begin with:

I. His great enjoyment of God's presence

He tells us of an hour in his life when he enjoyed unusual nearness to God, or when he was suddenly transported to the place where God dwells. It was a place of indescribable glory, where he saw and heard things, the wonderful and ravishing nature of which was utterly beyond speech. No words in our earthly vocabulary could convey what he had seen and heard in that upper world of bliss and glory. This unexpected and surprising experience might have happened in "the nigh watches", or during the hours of conscious activity, and whether he was in the body or out of the body he did not know. Only God knows.

The place where he found himself, he speaks of as "the third heaven". To Paul, as an Israelite, the first heaven is the place immediately above us–the sky where where the birds sing. And then there is the swesome astronomical heaven, the place where sun, moon and stars move in their own orbits. Beyond them all was the city of the Great King or the third Heaven. This is the place where elect angels and elect and redeemed men shall forever dwell in God's presence. He was in Heaven while he was still an inhabitant of time. Abraham, the father of the faithful sojourned for a season in Caanan, the place which God had given him a promise, and while as yet he had it but in the promise.

In Christ, and while we are still in this world, our citizenship is in Heaven. "We are come to Mount Zion, the city of the living God, the heavenly Jerusalem, and to an innumerable company of angels, to the general assembly and Church of the first-born written in Heaven, and to God the Judge of all, and to the spirits of just men made perfect." These words refer to the great privileges which belong to all those who are reconciled to God through the death of His Son, and who through Him, are established in a new and eternal relationship with God.

This wonderful experience in the life of Paul had happened fourteen years before he had written this epistle. It may have been shortly after his conversion–the time of his first love. Such seasons of unusual nearness to God have refreshed the lives of many of God's saints in all ages. It was not a unique enjoyment, although, on the other hand, many believers cannot say that, in their converse with God, they had reached such a height as Paul speaks of here. These Bethel hours are sweet beyond words. They are also vivid, solemn and memorable beyond all expression. Christ's three disciples could never forget the day when, with their Lord on the mount, they beheld His glory and heard the voice from the excellent glory, "This is my beloved Son in whom I am well pleased". We have come across some of God's people who had such seasons of solemn communion with God, though their experiences had their own different or peculiar spiritual contests.

We know that there are those who deprecate what they call the mystical side of Christian experience. They speak about Christian "subjectivism" as precarious at his best. We must never, they say, give any place to mere feelings. Dreams and visions have no significance or value.

It is certainly true that God's Word is the solid immoveable foundation of all true Christian experience and anything that deviates from God's infallible word should be dismissed as a mere empty cloud. On the other hand how can God's presence or the love of Christ dwell in our hearts without feeling? True faith is not a cold abstraction. It is the "substance of things hoped for". It often brings us a foretaste, or is the earnest, of those unspeakable blessings which are reserved for us in great fulness at God's right hand. We taste and see that God is good. Faith is a cup which, at times, is full and running over. By faith we also see the King in his beauty and the land of far distances. Our souls then say, "Whom have I in the heavens but thee, and there is none on earth that I desire besides Thee". Such enjoyments make us hope and long for the day when we shall see Him as He is. They also bring our souls into a dimension of spiritual existence unknown to a formal religion. At such times our souls rejoice in the Lord with joy unspeakable and full of glory. Then our love for God, His people, and Word deepen beyond words. And it is not a psychological impossibility to separate feelings, and even ecstacy, from such deep communion with God and with the eternal world. At such times our very sleep may be sweet to us, for as the Bible reveals, He can converse with us by His word in the night watches, "when deep sleep falleth upon men" as during the hours of consciousness. For all we know it may have been that like Jacob it was while asleep on his pillow that Paul found himself in Heaven with God. He evidently had no awareness of time or of anything pertaining to the world. But when it happened and how it happened, the Lord in His wisdom has concealed from us. We also may have our own precious spiritual memories which we cannot convey to our fellow creatures, and which we hide in our own hearts.

Let us now look at:

II. His great trial

One would think that if Paul would be safe anywhere, and beyond the reach of Satan and his temptations, it would be at this time. But Satan very often lays his snares on the highest pinnacle of Christian enjoyment. They say that the deepest parts of the ocean are often opposite the highest mountains. Many of God's people have discovered that their days of Heaven on earth are often a preparation for some severe trial, or are followed by some distressing conflicts. John Bunyan descended into the valley of humiliation where he met the great adversary, Apollyon, who threw his fiery darts into his soul, after spending a blissful season in the House Beautiful and in the company of those who loved God. It is on the heights that we need to watch our footsteps, and exercise more caution lest we fall.

In the Scottish Highlands there was a godly man who, during one of the local Communion seasons was favoured with much of the Lord's presence. For several days the dew of Hermon rested on his soul. His spiritual consolation was indescribable. As he was returning home he met a friend who asked him how it fared with him on the mount of ordinance. His answer was that for several days he felt as if he had been in Heaven. His friend then made the remark that he would now need for a good number of days to endure much of the hatred of Hell. And so it was. It was after the Holy Dove descended on our blessed Lord and the Voice from Heaven proclaimed that He was God's Beloved Son, that He was led by the Spirit into the wilderness where, for forty days and nights, He was tempted of the devil. Although as the eternal and unchangeable Son of God He had no sin, and could not sin yet He was tempted in all points like as we are. Paul, like all God's people, had now own share of the sufferings of Christ. The famous American preacher, Mr Edward Payson, spoke once of the great extreme of feeling to which he was subject. At one time he felt "caught up" with Paul and heard "things unutterable" while at other times, sunk to the lowest depth of depression, he felt that his very existence was a burden too heavy for him to bear.

The Lord permitted Satan to buffet his beloved servant lest the sin of pride should ensnare him as it did others of his contemporaries, and lest he should lose his Christian humility and his sense of utter dependence on his Lord for the grace of daily perseverance. He would also remind him that he was still in the flesh, and that his life here was a warfare against the powers of darkness. But what Paul especially discovered in this affliction was how much God loved him in bringing him back from the way of danger. And he permitted the vicious dog of hell to buffet him lest he should god further astray. "Whom the Lord loveth he chasteneth." "As many as I love I rebuke and chasten."

What his thorn in the flesh was Paul does not tell us. Many views have been expressed on this subject. Some, if not most of these affirm that the thorn was some acute physical pain; but although he speaks of it as "in the flesh" it might on the other hadn have been some great spiritual trial. In all his epistles Paul never complains of his physical afflictions. Rather does he glory in them. Satan also can use evil men and women to grieve our spirits. These, indeed, may prove to be the messengers of Satan. And is there not something very edifying in Paul's concealment of the source of his trial? Who knows, dear friend but it may be the very thorn which is at the root of your own trial or affliction? We cannot tell.

Our time of pain or trial often brings to light the kind of people we are. As Christ in the parable of the sower tells us there are some who assume a fair religious complexion till they come into contact with some acute adversity—and then the mask comes off to reveal that God's word had never taken root in their heart, and that the love of God was not in them. We have known some such men who tried to drown or forget their sorrow in drink or in following the vanities of this world. But in the day of adversity God's child has only one place and one person to whom he may resort. He kneels at the Throne of Grace and seeks the help of God alone. "For this," says Paul "I prayed the Lord thrice that it might depart from me." The word thrice used here does not necessarily mean that he just prayed three times; but rather that he wrestled often or persistently with God for help. And there was no immediate answer from God. This added to his burden and distress. It is, indeed, a bitter drop in the cup of God's child when He remains silent to his cry. This has often happened in the lives of the saints. "O! that I knew where I might find Him" was the cry of Job. "How long" said David "wilt though forget me, O Lord? For ever? How long wilt thou hide thy face from me?" Was not this also a bitter drop in Christ's own cup of sufferings. "O, my God, I cry in the day time, but thou hearest not; and in the night season and I am not silent."

It may be that God delayed His answer to Paul's prayer because, in his distress, his prayer was not in harmony with His holy will. He sought deliverance from his great pain; but God refused to do this. Instead, and for his own eternal good, He was to give him strength to endure it. This then brings us to our next and last thought, which is:

III. His great Triumph and Comfort

We notice that this comfort, and reconciliation to God's will, came through a prayer which was specifically addressed to Christ, the Brother born in adversity. We may pray to any of the Persons in the Godhead, for each is equal to the others in power and glory. Paul knew that His exalted Lord was the only mediator between him and God. He also knew that in all his afflictions He was afflicted, and that before He was crowned with many crowns in the higher realms of glory He bore on His head a crown of thorns. It was a crown that was symbolic of the many agonies which all His life He had to endure both in His sould and body. "Truly, he hath borne our griefs and carried our sorrows." "He was tempted in all points like as we are yet without sin." Though He is now and eternally beyond all personal sufferings, He is still touched with a feeling of our infirmity. Whatever depths we come into, He was, as our substitute, there before us. Besides, the Church which is His mystical body and the apple of His eye, is so united to Him in love that her sufferings cannot be dissociated from Him. Could Paul ever forget that moment when, on the way ot Damascus to slaughter His saints, he heard a voice from heaven, "Saul, Saul why persecutest thou *me*?" And although Christ forgave him his sin in touching His loved ones, Paul never forgot. It was that voice from Heaven that made him realise the depth of love and pity that was in the heart of the Lord toward His suffering people. In his own sufferings, therefore, it was to Christ he went for the needed help.

Christ, we notice, sent His help to him through His word. "And he said unto me, my grace is sufficient for thee, for my strength is made perfect in weakness." Our Lord is He who has that tongue of the learned that he might know "how to speak a word in season to him that is weary". As the universe is upheld by the word of His power, so also is the new spiritual creation. All His people are kept by His power through faith unto salvation. A word from His mouth is better than a thousand from any other lips. His sheep hear His voice, they know His voice, and they love His voice. "The voice of my Beloved." If His voice is sweet to His people so is their voice to Him. "O my dove that art in the cleft of the rock and in the secret places of the stair let me see thy countenance, let me hear thy voice; for sweet is thy voice and they countenance is comely." How sweet was Paul's voice to Christ when in the secret place he poured out his heart and tears before Him in prayer. If the voice of Christ was sweet to Paul so also was the blessing which accompanied His word: "My grace is sufficient for thee; for my strength is made perfect in weakness."

One would have thought that with such a wonderful enjoyment of God's presence such as he had in the third heaven, Paul would have the strength to withstand every trial as long as he lived. But it was not so. All the people of God know that they need Christ's grace for each and every day. "As thy day so shall thy strength be." Passing as we do—spiritually speaking—through a great wilderness, yesterday's manna will not suffice us for today. Our prayer should be: "Give us this day our daily bread." All the grace that we need is in Christ alone. "Of His fullness have all we received and grace for grace." Each day we should pray that a wave of this grace from the infinite ocean of His fullness should reach our souls and sustain us to the end. And it matters not what depths of affliction we may come into, His grace is always sufficient and ever available. It is through the channels of our weakness that our Lord communicates His grace to us. "My strength is made perfect in weakness."

The word grace in this verse may be translated, "love". The link between grace on earth and glory in Heaven is unbreakable, for we cannot be separated from the love of Christ. Satan, with all his wiles, power and hatred never discovered a way or devised means whereby this could be done. Christ who has all power in heaven and on earth is Himself present within the grace which He gives. "*My* grace." Christ within us is the hope of glory, and this hope shall never be put to shame because the love of Christ is shed abroad in our hearts.

But, dear friends, as long as you are in this world you must, like Paul, live with your own thorn. The day, however, is near hand when sorrow and sighing shall for ever flee away. Soon we shall be gathered into the garden above where there is no more pain, and where the sweet air of eternal peace shall waft through our beings and where also the Day Star shall arise in our hearts—to go down no more. All who inhabit that glorious world are a people who came out of great tribulation, but who by the grace of God overcame every enemy and endured to the end. Happy indeed are the people whose God is the Lord. Amen.

LOVE'S UNCONQUERABLE RESOLVE

"*And Ruth said, Intreat me not to leave thee, or to return from following after thee: for whither thou goest, I will go; and where thou lodgest, I will lodge, thy people shall be my people, and thy God my God*"–Ruth, Ch. 1, v. 16

Naomi spent ten years in the land of Moab. These were mostly, and within the sphere of God's providence, years of desolation and sorrow. In that alien land she had stood by the graves of her husband and her two sons. But however great her trials she remained a bright witness for God in a place of spiritual darkness. She did not adapt herself to the ways of a godless and idolatrous people. It is obvious from the context that the candle of true piety graced her home there. Our homes are often a commentary on the worth of our Christian profession. By her life and conversation she was the means of bringing at least one soul to the knowledge of the only true God. Through her witness and prayers, Ruth, her daughter-in-law, became a bright spiritual ornament for God. And who can estimate the far-reaching results of this one conversationto Christ. Christ, according to the flesh, was a direct descendant of this young, widowed woman and of Boaz, her second husband. Besides, these words of hers, spoken to her mother-in-law at the crossroads of destiny, are laden with immortal beauty. They are both a plea and a sincere confession of her faith in the only living and true God. They are words, we believe, which have been the means of bringing many souls to the Lord. And they shall continue to speak to the generations to come. They are also expressive of the deep and pure love which was in her heart to God and His people. As we look at these words of Ruth let us consider:

I. Her willing and final separation from a godless world

In the case of Ruth, as in that of her sister-in-law, there was every natural reason as to why she should return to her native place. Her people and their gods were still there. There also was her husband's grave. And beside her stood her weeping sister-in-law who had hitherto shared many of her joys and sorrows. And her earthly prospects were bleak in the extreme. Like her mother-in-law, death had taken away all her natural supports. Her temporal state is reflected in the words of Naomi: "I went out full and the Lord hath brought me home again empty." But perhaps a more trying test, and a greater inducement against her separation from her land, her gods and her people, were Naomi's own words. More than once she pleaded with her to return to her native place and home. But it was all to no avail. While Orpah went back, Ruth "clave unto her". Her decision was final. She had put her false religion and her old ways behind her back for ever. "And when Naomi saw that she was stedfastly minded to go with her, then she left speaking unto her."

As with many of His people, the Lord put Ruth through a severe testing at the very beginning of her spiritual pilgrimage. Many were the nominal followers of our Lord in this world; but when, by His Word, He who had His fan in His hand, put them to the test, most of them, like chaff, moved away to return no more. "From that time many of His disciples went back and walked no more with Him. Then said Jesus unto the twelve, Will ye also go away? Then Simon Peter answered Him, Lord to whom shall we go? Thou hast the words of eternal life." Like Christ's true disciples, Ruth's attachment to Naomi and her God was not something merely natural or sentimental or which stood related to congenial earthly prospects. It went deeper than mere nature. It was, in fact, the evidence that she was now a new creature in Christ, and that the Holy Spirit had wrought a work of grace in her heart–making her willing in a day of His power; willing, not only to follow the Lord in the day of ease, but also in the day of adversity. Like Lydia, her lovely spiritual counterpart spoken of in the Book of Acts, the Lord had drawn her to Himself with the cords of love. He had opened her heart that there He might dwell for evermore. She had by faith seen the King in His beauty and had heard His voice calling her away to a heavenly and better country with Himself. She had also tasted in her soul of His unspeakable love. From that hour her affections were set on the things which are spiritual and eternal. She was led into the path of righteousness to walk "in the footsteps of the flock", and to share both the afflictions and the joys of her Lord and His people. This is the witness that lies inherent in her words as, in her great resolve, she embraced Naomi and her God, and set her face toward the land of Israel. It may be that Orpah's interest in the God and people of Israel was apparently as real as that of Ruth. It was in the hour of crisis that the inward, or spiritual, difference between them came to light. Christ's parable of the sower is truly an awe-inspiring comment on the difference between the spurious follower of the Lord and the true. But in many cases only the Coming Day shall reveal to what category we belong. The separation of God's people from their former ways and follies implies a choice of something of infinitely greater value and satisfaction. It was so in the case of Ruth.

Look then for a moment at:

II. Her Wise and Everlasting Choice

Her choice at its highest level was, in the first place, of God Himself. Did she know, as a mere child in the faith, that her choice of the God of Abraham, the blessed and eternal I AM, was because He had chosen her in His well-beloved Son from all Eternity, and that before the world was He had espoused her to Himself within the covenant of grace? Perhaps she did; for "the secret of the Lord is with them who fear Him and He will show unto them His covenant". The assurance of God's choice of us in Christ is precious beyond words. But our choice of Him, though it has its ultimate source in His own electing love, is also precious to Him beyond all that we can ever know. This is one of the sweet mysteries of God's sovereign grace. He loved us that we might love Him, and that we might enjoy Him in His love for ever.

We could say of Ruth that the words which our Lord spoke of Mary in the home in Bethany, as she sat at His feet drinking in the words of everlasting life, could be applied to her also. She had made choice of the one thing needful, the good part, that would never be taken from her. Boaz, her future husband and a man of God, knew the genuineness of her choice and witness when he spoke to her as one whose trust was in the Lord God of Israel under whose wings she had made her dwelling place for evermore.

Like Ruth, a fundamental mark of all true believers is discovered in their love to God. "The righteous love Thee." "Thou knowest Lord that I love Thee." "We love Him because He first loved us." All His people on earth and in Heaven could utter these same words. The end for which God created us was that we might love Him with all our mind, heart, soul and strength. Our love to God we show by our obedience to His Will. In a state of sin man does the reverse of this. We hate Him without a cause, and rebel against all His commandments. The new creation, however, is given the will, the grace and the power to conform, and finally to attain, to this His claim upon us. It was her love to God that therefore comes to light in Ruth's great resolve.

Why do we love the Lord? Do we not love Him supremely for what He is in Himself? In all His glorious attributes He is infinitely desirable, precious, and "altogether lovely" to His own people. Throughout eternal ages we shall go on making ever new and enrapturing discoveries of His glory; but since His glory, majesty and love are infinite, or "past finding out", we can only stand in awe, in wonder, in ecstasy and adoration in His presence for ever. We love Him for the innumerable proofs which He has given us, and which He shall continue to give us, of His love to us. These proofs of His love all meet in the Gift of His Beloved Son who gave Himself for us. "For He that spared not His own Son but delivered Him up for us all, how shall He not with Him also freely give us all things?" But as this love is also personal, all the people of God make their own discoveries of God's love to them in Christ. With Paul each of them may say, "The Son of God who loved me and gave Himself for me."

Do we not love Him also in all that He permits and does, both in His judgments upon the world and in His personal dealings with ourselves. Does He punish the wicked? Does He chastise His people for their many and frequent backslidings? In these we see His holiness and justice. In His chastisements we see His love for us. "Whom the Lord loveth He chasteneth, and scourgeth every son Whom He receiveth." "Though He slay me yet will I trust in Him." It is a love which the waters of affliction can never drown. "Love never faileth."

Those who love and make choice of the Triune God, love His people also. It is a spiritual impossibility to love the One and not to love the other. Those who love Him by whom we are begotten, love those who are begotten of Him. "We know that we have passed from death to life because we love the brethren." This is the sum and substance of Christ's new commandment to all who are His. "A new commandment I give unto you, that ye love one another." When the apostle Peter stood before the Lord, where in answer to His questions he made a threefold profession of his love to Him, he was commanded to manifest or to prove his love by feeding His sheep and His lambs. And this he truly did by his care for His flock as long as he lived. In all their sufferings his love toward them never abated for a moment. The law of Christ is that we should bear the burdens of His people and comfort them in their many tribulations. Ruth knew the sorrows that lodged in the heart of Naomi and how she was given the waters of Marah to drink. And it was this that united her heart to her in much tenderness. Moses chose rather to suffer affliction with the people of God than to enjoy all the pleasures of sin for a season. A man once stood before the Lord and uttered these words in his prayer: "Lord I love Thee because Thou hast loved Thy people; and I love them because they love Thee." Ruth's love to Naomi brings back to our memory an anecdote about a gracious but timid young woman who, on her way to church on a Communion Sabbath morning, saw a number of God's people in front of her on the road. Instantly these words deeply touched her spirit: "Who are these that fly as a cloud, and as doves to their windows?" With these words she also felt an indescribable love for them surfacing within her being. It was a love that remained with her all her days. "Thy people shall be my people."

When we make choice of God and His people we also make choice of His, and their, way. "Whither thou goest, I will go." David's great prayer, as expressed in the 119th Psalm, was that he might be led to the end in the way of truth, in the way of holiness, or in the straight and narrow way that leads to the Jerusalem which is above. The great evidence of being in the paths of righteousness is that God Himself is our Companion in the way. "And Enoch walked with God." God's people are not always conscious of His gracious presence, but are there not sweet seasons in their life when by the enjoyment of His presence they know that He is beside them? He warms their heart with His love, and makes them long for the day when He shall no more be "as a wayfaring man that turneth aside to tarry for a night."

As the Psalmist could rejoice in having the Lord as his Companion on his pilgrimage journey he was also the companion of those who loved him. "I am a companion of all them that fear Thee, and of them that keep Thy precepts." Those who follow the Shepherd are in the footsteps of His flock. Bunyan's Pilgrim had quite a few fake companions in the way, but because they knew not the Lord they, allured by other false ways and carnal interests, went aside and perished in their ignorance. But, as Ruth followed Naomi, *Hopeful* remained with him to the end, both in sunshine and storm, till they both reached their happy Home above.

We notice also that Ruth, in her great decision, said to Naomi that her place of abode would also be hers. "Where thou lodgest, I will lodge."

although God's people have here, as we said, but the tabernacle of a way-faring man, God has provided them with places of rest both in Himself and within the bosom of His church. He is the dwelling place of His people in all generations. He is "a little sanctuary" to them in their days of weakness and loneliness. God Himself rests in His Zion. "This is my rest for ever: here will I dwell; for I have desired it." And where He rests there they rest also. When David was isolated from God's house he envied even the sparrow and the swallow which rested and made their nests in its secret corners. Is there any place on earth more endearing to the gracious soul than the public means of grace, especially when they know that "the Lord is there".

"How lovely is Thy dwelling place
O Lord of hosts, to me!
The tabernacles of Thy grace
how pleasant, Lord, they be!" (Ps. 84.)

We knew of some, who, conscious of God's presence in the means of grace, felt that they would have stayed there for ever. There, spiritually speaking, God's people lodge together with Jesus "in the midst". "Where two or three are gathered together in My Name there am I." Alas, He is not always there. Our places of worship may, because of our sins and prayerlessness, become places of cold spiritual desolation. But the communion of saints may be enjoyed with "the two or three", or even alone in the secret place and under the banner of Christ's love. But, however, and wherever, His people are in this world, the Lord has decreed that they shall eternally dwell together in His house of many mansions above. Neither death nor life shall separate them from His love, or break the bond that binds them together in their glorious Redeemer. A man once said: "The Lord's people shall never say farewell to one another for the last time." Naomi and Ruth are now happy and together in the presence of Him where there is a fullness of joy and with the spirits of just men made perfect.

Consider, in the last place:

III. Her Great Reward

Boaz, in addressing Ruth, said: "The Lord recompense thy work, and a full reward be given three of the Lord God of Israel."

Her reward was not, in the true sense, what came to her within the sphere of Providence. God did supply all her temporal needs. The ripe and wholesome grain from the fields of Boaz was put at her disposal. Not only so, but Boaz treated her with great kindness, respect and affection. He did not disown the relationship into which she came to him through the death of her first husband, who was his near relation. And in obedience to one of God's kindly laws he espoused her to himself.

But these favours only touched her momentary temporal life in this world. Her spiritual and eternal reward was infinitely of greater value. And it came to her not through any dispositional kindness or personal merit, but entirely, as we said, through the sovereign gace of God. God shall reward all His people at last; but they all know that all their blessings have their source in Him who alone is their Righteousness and whose merits are infinite. David said that in the keeping of God's law there is "a great reward"; but he knew that out of Christ he deserved nothing and could have done nothing. Ruth's access to the unsearchable riches of Christ, and her relationship to Him as her spiritual Husband, were of God's sovereign grace. As Boaz supplied her temporal needs God supplied all her needs according to His riches in glory by Jesus Christ. She was provided with the living Bread which came down from Heaven, with "the finest of the wheat". Christ, who has a fullness of grace and truth, shall be the life of His people for ever and ever. But who can know how great is His goodness laid up, or reserved in Heaven, for all who fear Him? "The half has never yet been told." This reward is, indeed, the greatest that God could have bestowed on His people. It is nothing less than Himself. "Fear not Abraham I am thy shield and thy exceeding great reward." As a daughter of Abraham this was supremely's Ruth's reward also.

And as Boaz claimed Ruth as his own bride, after the law relative to this matter had been satisfied before many witnesses, so Christ, who satisfied God's law and justice as their Surety and Substitute, and to whom these give infallible witness that this was done, claims His Church as His own. Her first husband had died and she died in him; but He is the second husband who died for her and passed by her and said, "Live". He also speaks to her in these words: "Thou art mine." Thou art mine because I loved thee and made choice of thee from all eternity. I have purchased thee with My blood, and called thee effectually out of darkness into light. "I have formed thee for Myself." "Thou are mine" for thou also has chosen me to be thine for ever. Thy voice is, "My Beloved is mine and I am His." Dear friend, have you left the far country, or your city of Destruction? Are you a Ruth or an Orpah? Is Christ the Beloved of your soul? O, pray with all who are His:

"Remember me, Lord, with that love
which Thou to thine dost bear;
With Thy salvation, O my God,
to visit me draw near:

"That I Thy chosen's good may see,
and in their joy rejoice;
And may with thine inheritance
triumph with cheerful voice." (Ps. 106.)

Amen.

THE EMMAUS WALK

"But they constrained him, saying, abide with us for it is toward evening and the day is far spent. And he went in to tarry with them"–St Luke, Ch. 24, v. 29

There are few things more impressive than the spiritual calm with which the Gospels end. Our Lord's sufferings are now over. The fearful scenes which marked His death on the Cross have come to an end. The "dogs" and the "bulls of Bashan" which, in the figurative words of the Psalm, compassed Him about have, for the time being, ceased to bark and roar. Unknown to themselves all His enemies on earth and in hell are for ever overcome. Sin is destroyed and the grave is robbed of its prey.

During those forty days between His resurrection and ascension our Lord was not seen by any carnal or unconverted eyes. But the recurring and sweet surprises of His manifestations to His own people all tell their own wonderful story. Among those who were privileged to see the Lord at that time were Cleopas and his friend, who, under a burden of sorrow, were on the way to the village of Emmaus. There are several things which we might relate to this event and on which I should like to dwell. Let me say a word, first, on:

I. How the Lord came into their company

He came when they were in a state of much anxiety and bewilderment. As their Lord afterwards told them, this sad state had it source in their unbelief and their ignorance of the Scriptures. Throughout all the years of His ministry our Lord had been telling His disciples all that would befall Him in the accomplishment of His great work. He must suffer and die. He was to be rejected of His nation and lifted up on a Cross of agony and shame. The sign of His Messiahship which He was to give the world was the sign of the prophet Jonah. For three days he was to lie in the grave, and then arise again in His own power and for the justification of all His people. All this was predicted of Him in the "volume of the Book". As we know the supreme witness of the Spirit in the Word has to do with the sufferings of Christ and the glory that should follow these. But Israel, generally speaking, followed another vision. They looked for a Messiah who would arrive on the scene in outward splendour, and who would exert His power in the temporal elevation and liberation of their nation. He would subdue all their political enemies. They looked for One who would conform to all their own traditions. So deeply had these unscriptural expectations influenced their minds that when our Lord spoke of His rejection and death even His own intimate followers could not believe or grasp His Words. It was Peter who said, "Far be it from Thee, Lord; this shall not be unto Thee."

And here we have Cleopas and his friend in a state of utter dismay over the unexpected and shameful death of their Lord. A mist of confusion rested on their minds.

Now, I do not wish to dwell, exclusively, on this solemn and deeply impressive historical event relating to thosetwo followers of Christ. What I want to say now is that, for various reasons, the Lord's people are often anxious and sad on their pilgrimage journey in this lower vale. Although their sorrows have their source in entirely different circumstances to those mentioned in this chapter, all of them have sorrows peculiar to themselves. It would be unwise to try to enumerate these for each knows the plague of his own heart and his own frequent perplexities. Our crosses, burdens and temptations may differ in many ways. These bring us to the Lord for the needed and promised grace given in the words "As thy days so shall thy strength be". And like Cleopas and his friend we sometimes share our burdens with one another. This is one of Christ's laws–that we should "bear one another's burdens". Christian fellowship and conversation are often of great value.

We are told of those who, in other days, feared the Lord and who often spake the one to the other. And the Lord hearkened and heard them. Their prayers and conversation reached His ear. His promise is that where the two or three meet together in His name He is there also to sustain them by His all-sufficient grace and gracious presence. The burden under which these two men sighed was known to Christ. It was this that brought Him to their side. He came to relieve them by His Word and Presence. When, like them, we are given the support of God's Word accompanied by a consciousness of His nearness to us, we come to know what true comfort is.

But with His word of comfort came also His *word of rebuke.* "O fools and slow of heart to believe all that the prophets have spoken." God's people, who are all in His school, are sometimes poor scholars. He speaks to them both by His Word and in His providence, but they are often slow of understanding. The sin of unbelief may often bring them into depths of depression. To these two, the awesome events relating to the death of Christ could not be reconciled with their own expectations, or with their own interpreptation of the Scriptures. Within the context of our own life are we ourselves not often in similar straits? Although we know that God's Word is infallible, and that all which happens within the sphere of his providence has been decreed from all eternity, yet we sometimes fail to believe what the Lord tells us with respect to both. He assures us that all things shall work together for our good and that His Word, which is forever settled in the heavens, is changeless and can never pass away. But not only are we slow to believe, but we often anticipate that God is going to bring all to fulfilment according to our own expectations. But His ways are not our ways, neither are His thoughts our thoughts. Before His rebuke, these two men, like all His people, could only bow their heads. This humble acknowledgment of their ignorance was one evidence that they were truly His.

He came also into their company to *enlighten them in the knowledge of Himself.* Christ, as we said, is the substance of God's written Word. There He is set before us both in His humiliation and glory. "My Beloved," said the Church, "is white and ruddy; the chiefest among ten thousand." It was through the lattice of the promise that the Lord favoured them with a soul-warming glimpse of His glory which also revived their spirits. He who also "opened their understanding", is the prophet of His people. All His child-rent are taught of Himself. Therefore they pray: "Open my eyes, that of Thy law the wonders I may see." And the greatest wonder they behold in His Word is He whose name is *Wonderful.* The true knowledge of Christ in His mediatorial work, love and glory, is something which is eternally out-with the reach of the natural mind. It is also something which commands the supreme interest of His people. They say with Moses: "I shall now turn aside and see this great sight."

It is interesting to notice that while there was no natural recognition of Him as He walked by their side, their inner eyes, on the other hand, saw and recognised Him in the Word as the true Messiah of God. The Just, in other words, shall live by Faith and not be sight. "But we all; with open face beholding as in a glass the glory of the Lord, are changed into the same images from glory to glory, ever as by the Spirit of the Lord."

There was another reason why our Lord came into their company. It was *to confirm the reality of His resurrection.* The news of this had been conveyed to them from other friends, but now it was given to them to know personally that the Lord was risen indeed. The moment did indeed arrive when, at the end of their journey, they actually recognised Him, and when an infallible conviction possessed their spirit that it was the Lord. They then knew Him as the "One who liveth and was dead, and who is alive for evermore". They could say, "I know that my Redeemer liveth."

Although, dear friends, we shall never, like them, see Him in this life with our natural eyes, is not our spiritual apprehension of His glory as real and as sweet as if He literally stood by our side? It is with the eye of faith that we see "the King in His beauty".

Another characteristic of their experience was the suddenness and unex-pectedness of His coming into their company. It was not by any gradual process of reasoning on their part that the clouds which hung over them were dispelled, but by their Lord's sudden appearance at their side. Many of the Lord's people could speak of those sweet "surprises" when the Lord blesses them with His presence. Has not this often occurred in your own life? You might have been reading the Word, or on your knees in prayer. You might have been in the public means of grace or walking prayerfully by yourself in the way. He just came. You knew who it was. "It is the Lord." You might have said with Thomas "My Lord and My God", or with Jacob "The Lord is in this place". If these surprises are sometimes brief, they are also memorable and precious beyond words.

But notice now for a moment:

II. How His Word and Presence affected Them

"Did not your heart burn within us as He walked with us by the way. . ." These words show that through His coming they were revived in their souls. God's people may go for many days as if they were in the grip of a spiritual winter. They become conscious of coldness and hardness within their spirits. But how soon this may change! Whenever the Church in the Song heard the voice of her beloved, and when that voice touched her heart in reviving power, her winter season came to an end. "For, lo, the winter is past; the rain is over and gone; the flowers appear on the earth, the time of the singing of birds is come and the voice of the turtle is heard in our land."

Once I sat at the bedside of an old Christian man. The sun of his life in this world was going down behind a calm sea. As a young man he was brought under the power of the truth. The season of his first love was like a morning without a cloud. Gradually, however, his time of consolation declined, and he was left to mourn over "the years which the locust hath eaten". He was like one who had been long dead. Now it was toward evening and the day was far spent. But one day as he sat in a church the Word preached began to affect his heart. He was given a new spiritual morning. The Lord passed by and breathed upon him with the warm breath of His mouth. His affections, under the dew of heaven and under the rays of the Sun of Righteousness were revived. His heart burned within him. At eventide it was light. The sun arose on his soul to go down no more, for he passed, I believe, out of time on the lap of this wonderful spiritual enjoyment.

What these two were particularly conscious of at that hour was a deepening of their love to the Lord. The love of Christ in the heart is like a fire which many waters cannot quench. It was this that Job meant when he said: "Though He slay me, yet will I trust Him." How is this love born and sustained in the soul? Only by the knowledge of how He loved us. Christ, in opening to them the Scriptures, made them see how He loved them. They saw how, as their Substitute, He took their place on the accursed tree and drank that cup of woe which, otherwise, they would have to continue drunking for ever. It was this love that constrained Him to leave the mansions of glory, to inhabit a lost and fallen world where He had nowhere to lay His head. The "joy set before Him' as the joy that he would have in glorifying God by doing His will, and in having the subjects of His love with Him in heaven. "He shall see of the travail of His soul and shall be satisfied." He shall rejoice over His redeemed people as a bridegroom rejoiceth over his bride.

It was this knowledge that set their hearts aflame. "We love Him because He first loved us." It was this that moved Paul to exclaim: "The Son of God who loved me, and gave Himself for me." Love is the true response of the revived heart. Whatever we do, whatever we are, or whatever we give, if we are without charity, or love, we are nothing and we have nothing. Love alone never fails nor passes away. "Thou knowest Lord that I love Three", is a confession within the bosom of all who know the Lord. An old man was once asked how he felt on the threshold of eternity. "I know now," he answered, "that love is the element of heaven." This love, which is shed abroad in our hearts here, shall continue to deepen within us for ever, and we shall go on making fresh discoveries of its wonder in the ages to come. The true Christian life, as Jonathan Edwards was never weary of saying is "a matter of the affections". Knowledge in the mind, or religious formality in the life, can, without true love in our hearts become a destructive snare. In the Christian life. love and joy go together. Those who love Christ rejoice in Him with "joy unspeakable and full of glory". They rejoice in possessing Him. They rejoice in the prospect of being with Him where He is. They rejoice in his great and precious promises which shall have their perfect fulfilment by and by. Whatever sorrows may touch their life here, the source of their joy shall remain. It was this fact that so deeply impressed the pagan communities in which the early Christians witnessed and laboured. No suffering or deprivation quenched their joy in the Lord. When the Psalmist was beset with many trials he addressed his own spirit in these words: "Why art thou cast down, O my soul? and why art thou disquieted within me?" His one source of comfort was his coming to God his "exceeding joy" with all his cares. "In whom ye greatly rejoice, though now, for a season, if need be, ye are in heaviness through manifold temptations."

We believe, also, that their hearts burned within them with a desire to tell others what they themselves had seen and heard. "We cannot but apeak the things which we have seen and heard", was the answer of the disciples to those who would suppress their witness and silence their voice. "If these were to hold their peace the very stones would cry out." When Paul was brought to see the glory of the Redeemer and the great wonder of the forgiveness of all his sins, he said: "Lord what wilt thou have me to do?" From that hour, the love of Christ constrained him to proclaim the Gospel.

This is the holy dynamic within the soul of the true Church. This is what moves her to labour and suffer for Christ in this world. She has "good news" to tell to a perishing race. Those who taste of the love of Christ would have other to share their joy. "O, taste and see that God is good." These two, instead of going to rest after their long journey "arose up in the same hour" and went to Jerusalem to testify that they had seen the Lord. O, that this love, this joy and desire, might take possession of ourselves in our own day. We also have "good news from a far country." May the Lord give us the grace to value and proclaim it.

III. How He tarried with Them

Their enjoyment of the One who walked by their side was so deep and real that when they came to the end of the way, and when "He made as though he would have gone further" they constrained Him saying, "Abide with us for it is toward evening and the day is far spent." God's presence was so enrapturing and real to them that they refused to let Him go.

It is this enjoyment of God that unites His people together in love. This is the essence and the secret of the true communion of saints. This is a foretaste of Heaven on earth. The story was once told of two Christian friends who, along a quiet path, would accompany one another home. When the Lord would, through their Christian conversation, honour them with His presence, the way was all too short and they would continue "to see one another home" more than once. The Lord was their Companion.

In our text we see also the *sensitiveness of their spirit, and the reality of their discernment and concern.* When they felt that their Heavenly Friend might depart they constrained Him to tarry with them. God's people know when He is consciously with them. They can also tell, in the public means of grace, when and where His presence is vouchsafed or withheld. We once heard of a congregation which the Lord often honoured with His presence. It was the great concern of God's people there that He would not become a stranger in their midst. And whenever they felt that His power and presence were being withdrawn from the public means of grace they would gather together in secret and plead with Him not to leave them. "Abide with us" was their plea. They would also examine themselves lest, like Achan, any of them harboured some evil in their lives which might grieve the Spirit of the Lord. And in that corner of the vineyard He tarried while in other places He became a stranger.

With some of us here today it is, literally speaking, toward evening. Whether we are young or old in the faith we always need the Lord beside us. But only age brings its own infirmities and, perhaps, anxieties. It may also be associated with much loneliness. Some of our dear companions in the Lord who used to walk with us in the way are here no more. Their voices, their faces and smiles we shall neither see nor hear again in this world. But there is a never failing Friend. The Guide of our youth has promised to be the Godof our old age. "Cast me not off in time of old age; forsake me not when my strength faileth." His promise is, "I will never leave thee nor forsake thee."

Notice lastly–

IV. How He departed and yet remained

The inevitable moment did arrive when, in the breaking of bread, they recognised who their Companion was, "And their eyes were opened and they knew Him, and He vanished out of their sight." He vanished and yet He remained. He remained with them in His Word and promise. He remained with them in their own spiritual fellowship. His gracious presence would also stay with them to the end. The day will come in the life of all who love Him when He shall no longer vanish out of their sight. Here He often turns aside to tarry only for a night. Clouds sometimes take Him out of our sight, and we see but darkly through a glass. But the eternal day will soon break and all shadows shall for ever flee away. How sweet are the words– "Whom I shall see for myself and no another." This is what they often long for. "When shall I come and appear before God?" May God give us the heart and the walk of pilgrims and strangers in the earth. Each one of us should examine himself as to whether or not Christ is our Companion and whether or not we have the soul exercises and experiences of His people. Those who, like Enoch, walk with Him know that this great condescension on His part is a deep indisputable reality. "Nevertheless I am continually with thee." "His tabernacle is with men." He is not a stranger to His people, and for that reason He shall know and acknowledge them as His own in that day when He shall make up His jewels. Unless we know Christ as our Redeemer and Portion in this world of time we shall remain strangers to Him throughout eternity.

My dear Christless friends, are you walking on the solemn and brief journey to Eternity with your back to God, and it may be without any concern as to whether or not you shall ever savingly come to know Him? Listen to His words' "Look unto me and be ye saved." "Seek ye the Lord while He may be found, call ye upon Him while He is near." He is a God who "will abundantly pardon" all who return unto Him.

You may also constrain Christ to come into your heart and stay with you for ever. Then you will come to know Him in the wonder of His love and mercy. You will come to know Him as the altogether lovely One. Then you will never want to be separated from Him. "Abide with Me." And this He will do. He will abide with us for ever. He is the Friend that sticketh closer than a brother. He is easily entreated. And when, in answer to your prayer, He enters your heart to tarry with you for ever you shall come to know what true happiness is. "Happy art thou O Israel, O people saved by the Lord." O who can described the joy of ending life's journey resting in the bosom of Christ the Lover of our soul!

CONTINUING INSTANT IN PRAYER

"*Men ought always to pray and not to faint*"–Luke, Ch. 18, v. 1

The parable which our Lord uses here is meant to encourage God's people in all their trials and circumstances. If the unjust Judge answered and helped a poor persecuted woman because of her importunity and persistent annoyance, how much more will not God help and hear the cry of those whom He loves, and whom He pities more than a father pities his children? He may bear long with them, but His help and answer will come in His own time and way. Let us consider briefly:

I. The Duty here enforced or commended

"Men ought always to pray."

The word "ought" implies, as we know, an obligation. To pray, in other words, is a divine command. God exhorts us in His Word to "pray without ceasing", and to "continue instant in prayer". He commands us to "pray always with all spiritual prayer and supplication in the Spirit". Some of us recall the story of a good man who was beginning his spiritual pilgrimage, and who was somewhat perturbed by these words. How, he mused, could any man "pray without ceasing"? How could we do this when our necessary daily tasks demanded so much of our time? On this subject he decided to consult an older and a much exercised Christian man. When he approached this man's home he saw that he was digging part of his small croft. In answer to his question as to how he was, the older friend said–"I am here, digging and praying." The man then knew that our hearts could be engaged in prayer and our souls in communion with God while our hands were busy in this world.

As the natural breath which moves in our body is one evidence that we are physically alive, the breath of prayer within our souls is a proof that we are quickened by the Holy Spirit. God's Spirit dwells within His people as the Spirit of grace and of supplications. Prayer is the living link between a living God and a living soul.

This duty was one which our Lord Himself constantly observed. In this way also He left us an example that we should follow in His steps. Though He knew no sin, and although He was incapable of sinning, His life here, in the infirmities of our nature, was one of constant dependence on and communion with the Father. The Gospels tell us that there were times when He spent whole nights in prayer. He speaks prophetically in the Psalm–"In the night season I am not silent." Although some of His prayers are recorded in the Gospels–like His great prayer of intercession and the prayers which He uttered in Gethsemene and on the cross–most of them were only heard in heaven and offered in secret. And within the veil as our great High Priest in the upper sanctuary, He is, till the last of His people are home, making continual intercession for us.

If, as our Lord tells us, our life here is one of constant warfare with the powers of darkness the spiritual weapon of "all prayer" is essential to our preservation. Our enemies are many and subtle. They are in hell, they are in the world and they are within our own heart. There is the sin that doth so easily beset us. We are hated of all men who are strangers to God. And our adversary the devil goes about seeking whom he may devour. Our greatest conflicts are not against mere men, but against invisible principalities and powers, or against spiritual wickedness in high places. When Paul descended from the bliss of the third heaven, he was severely buffeted by Satan. But on his knees, and sustained by God's grace, he could say with God's prophet—"Rejoice not against me, O mine enemy: when I fall I shall rise again; when I sit in darkness the Lord shall be a light unto me." No weapon is more terrifying and more damaging to Satan than the prayers of the saints. It is in answer to prayer that God plucks His arm from His bosom both to nullify his designs and bring destruction to his kingdom and utter confusion to his emissaries. When the believer is personally assailed by his temptations and fiery darts, let him come to God in prayer. Let him ask his almighty advocate in heaven to help him. Then, according to His promise, as in the case of Joshua the high priest, help will come from above. "And the Lord said unto Satan, The Lord rebuke thee, O Satan; even the Lord that hath chosen Jerusalem rebuke thee: is not this a brand plucked out of the fire?" By God's rebuke the fiery darts of Satan were quenched, and the soul of His servant which was in the grip of fear was wrapped in peace and clothed with the garment of praise.

Do not our spiritual needs also demand unceasing prayer? It is not enough to have a sword in the hand if, at the same time, we are enfeebled through lack of spiritual nourishment. A good soldier must not only be well armoured but he must also be well fed. In this world we are passing through a great wilderness, where thirst and hunger often bring faintness into our souls. And for the soul that is born from above there is nothing in this world to meet its needs. Only the spiritual world can supply the needs of the spiritual man. Therefore, it is written—"But my God shall supply all your needs according to His riches in glory by Christ Jesus." In our Father's house—and nowhere else—there is bread enough and to spare. Christ is the hidden Manna from Heaven. He is also the smitten Rock from which flows the river of life which makes His Zion glad.

Our daily prayer should, therefore, be—"Ever more give us this bread." When Elijah, in a state of depression, discouraged by his enemies and by gross idolatry, asked God to take away his life, he was told by his angel who stood beside him "arise and eat" for a great journey was still before him. His work and witness for the Lord were not yet accomplished. And in the strength of the fare which God had provided for him he went for forty days and forty nights till he came to Horeb the mount of God. God, in answer to our prayer to give us each day our daily bread and to refresh us with a drink from the well of Bethlehem, will enable us to go from strength to strength until we appear before Him in Zion. So ought men always to pray.

If we are enlightened by God's Spirit, or are the children of the day, we ought always to pray that we may grow in grace and "in the knowledge of Christ." Some of God's greatest saints went to eternity with their heads bowed conscious of their poor spiritual attainments. It was holy Agar who said—"Surely I am more brutish than any man . . . I have neither learned wisdom not have the knowledge of the holy." Asaph confronted with his own ignorance of God's ways breathed out these words from a contrite heart—"So foolish was I and ignorant; I was as a beast before thee." We are of yesterday and know nothing or only in part. "For now we see through a glass darkly." Like King David our prayer always should also be:

"Open mine eyes that of thy law,
Thy wonders I may see."

But the prayers of the Church of God touch areas beyond the personal level. In our own day as we view the state of the world and God's cause, we cannot but tremble. Only the other day I had a letter from a godly lady in Canada in which she said that we were, without any doubt, "the generation of God's wrath" who were rapidly ripening for judgment. It is, therefore, a time that demands our constant vigilance, our unceasing prayers and our Christian withness. God's prophet, when he was told that the Lord was to exercise His holy indignation in the punishment of wicked men, both in the nation and within the church, earnestly prayed that in the midst of wrath He would still remember mercy. Abraham prayed that God would spare Sodom for the sake of "the remnant" that might still be there. But as they were all, apart from "just Lot", given over to unspeakable wickedness, His wrath could not be restrained. Are we, as a nation, blessed in the past with spiritual light and privileges of which Sodom knew nothing, going to be brought low? Yes, we are. This, dear friends, is therefore a time when we ought always to pray. "Arise, O Lord, and plead the cause that is thine own." "Thy kingdom come. Thy will be done in earth, as it is in heaven." The Word of God is replete with such pleas as these. Let us, therefore walk in the footsteps of God's people in every age who kept not silent, however great the evils by which they were surrounded.

Look now at:

II. The extent of our observance of this duty

"Men ought *always* to pray." I emphasise this word so as to bring out more clearly a peculiarity of true Christian experience. It is an experience which came to light in the lives of all the saints, both as recorded in the Bible and in Christian biography and testimony. These tell us that there are seasons in our lives when it is easy to pray—seasons when we are conscious of the drawing power of God's love, when His presence is with us, or when, in the words of Thomas Goodwin, we enjoy His smile. At such times the golden sceptre of His favour and promise is extended toward us. We seem to hear His voice saying to our soul—"What is thy request and what is thy desire." At such times we say—"Lord, it is good for us to be here." "This is God's house. This is the gate of heaven." How easy then does the stream of prayer flow from the heart and lips. But it is not always so.

Sometimes, if not often, we kneel in the presence of God under heavy burdens. We may be subject to many temptations, and conscious of spiritual desertion. With the Church we say—"Saw ye Him whom my soul loveth?" Or with the Psalmist we cry—

"How long wilt thou forget me, Lord
Shall it forever be?
O how long shall it be that thou
Wilt hide thy face from me?"

There are even times when there may be a sinful aversion to this duty within our souls. Those who work in the Lord's vineyard are sometimes under a cloud of depression and discouragement because they "see not their signs". With God's prophet they say—"I have laboured in vain, and spent my strength for naught."

And are there not seasons when within the personal sphere many providences bring us our night of weeping? "Against me," said Jacob, "are all these things." In the days of his heavy trials David wished that he had "the wings of a dove" that he might fly to some place of rest where he could escape from his sorrows. But as long as we are in this life the waters of Marah will be in our cup. "In this world ye shall have tribulation."

But our obedience to this command must remain unaffected by our present state. Our Lord uses the word "always" to remind us that whatever state we are in we ought to pray. Is it not true that our greatest blessings come to us through our sorrows? Was there ever a night in the life of Jacob more distressing than when he crossed the brook Jabbok and wrestled with God in prayer? He had no human power to resist what his alienated earth-bound brother might do to him as be moved toward him with four hundred men. Across the brook were all his helpless loved ones. Would Esau bathe his sword in his and their blood? Then it happened. God, the Angel of the Covenant, stood beside him. And he refused to let Him go till He would bless him. And bless him He did. His storm was changed to calm. As God restrained Laban from touching him He made his brother Esau to speak kindly to him. "He had power with the Angel and prevailed." He became a prince with God. The great blessing which streamed through his being in that hour reformed and sanctified his life beyond what he had hitherto known. Jacob became Israel. The prayers which are born of affliction have often brought us nearer to God than any other. A Scottish divine once remarked that it often happened with him that those prayers which begin with a sigh often ended with a song.

Let me now make a comment on:

III. The state against which we are warned

We are "not to faint." While this word may be expressive of one of our common infirmities it is, on the other hand, a state which we cannot isolate from sin, and especially from the sin of unbelief. We know that some of God's mighty men did faint in the day of adversity. John the Baptist, who in the beginning of his ministry spoke of the Messiah as God's Incarnate and well Beloved Son, as the Lamb of God and as the glorious Bridegroom for whom His church had been waiting in the exercise of faith and prayer, fainted in the day of trial. Unbelief took possession of his soul. "Art thou He that should come or look we for another?" But if we faint in the day of adversity our strength is small. When we are confronted with deep personal troubles, we may ask the question—"Who is sufficient for these things?" There is, however, our final answer to this question—"Our sufficiency is of God." This is, indeed, one of the supreme reasons why we should not faint in any situation.

The Lord whom we follow and serve has all power in heaven and on earth. "He shall not fail nor be discouraged until He hath set judgment in the earth." He is our almighty King. The storms of life may be very severe:

"But yet the Lord that is on high
Is more of might by far,
Than noise of many waters is
Or great sea billows are."

The Lord is going to exercise His power in a twofold way. By the rod of His power He is going to bring destruction upon the kingdom of darkness, and upon all who refuse to obey Him. Satan and his emissaries parade through our world in these dark and ugly times with their mouths uttering defiance against the Most High. "Who is God that we should obey Him?" "God is dead." God's appeal to evil men, as expressed, for example, in another Psalm, is often ignored and derided—"Be wise O ye kings: be instructed ye judges of the earth. Serve the Lord with fear. Kiss the Son lest He be angry, and ye perish from the way when His wrath is kindled but a little." The alternative to their obedience to God's command is their utter destruction. All His enemies shall at last "lick the dust" and shall melt away as "the fat of rams". If the power of His wrath is so terrible, the benign power which He is going to exercise in the revival and upbuilding of His Zion is both irresistible and glorious. Christ is going to extend the rod of His great power out of Zion. He is going to arise and have mercy upon her. Her time of favour, we believe, is near at hand. After evil men are consumed out of the earth the Sun of Righteousness is to arise upon His Church with healing in his wings. The wilderness and the solitary place shall then blossom as the rose. Our world shall be graced with men and women on whom the beauty of the Lord shall rest, and in whose hearts love to the Lord and to one another shall predominate. David ended his immortal prayers by anticipating the longed-for day when Christ's glory would fill the whole earth. Yes, we, in the light of Scripture, believe in a millenia age when God's power shall subdue the forces of evil which may cause us to faint today, and when men shall rejoice in the enjoyment of His spiritual presence and in constant communion with Him. Then it shall be said of all places where His people meet—"The Lord is there."Let this be our constant prayer—"Thy will be done on earth, as it is in heaven." The Lord would not have commanded us to plead with Him thus unless that day is coming. Like Moses on the top of Pisgah, do we not at times see, though only through a glass darkly when again Christ's church shall look forth as the morning and shall be fair as the moon under a clear and cloudless sky?

While such a sure promise and hope cannot but gladden our hearts, we may in the present hour and for various reasons feel downcast, but "In the Lord Jehovah is everlasting strength". And this strength which is in God He is able to communicate to all His people. In reliance on this grace, or strength, the weaker we are, the stronger we may be! Like Paul, let us glory in our infirmities that the power of Christ may rest upon us. With this grace which is all-sufficient and ever available, we should not faint. "Be strong in the Lord and in the power of His might." We believe that in the upper world of glory there are many of those who carry the palms of victory in their hand and who, on earth, were inclined to faint in the day of adversity, and who sometimes feared that they could not endure to the end. But they "overcame through the blood of the Lamb and through the words of their testimony".

In this parable Christ would have us know that His delays in answering our prayers are not denials. He may bear long with us, but answer us He will in His own time and way. By His delays He may try our faith, but not deny His promise. The lives of many of God's choice saints have, in this connection, their own story to tell. Think of how long God delayed the fulfilment of His promise to Abraham. What adverse providence and long delays did Jacob pass through before God answered his prayers! "I have waited for thy salvation, O Lord" was his last ecstatic utterance in this world. And it was David who said–"I had fainted unless I had believed to see the goodness of the Lord in the land of the living." We read in the Song of Solomon of the Church's holy resolve to wait, in the exercise of faith, patience and prayer, for the coming of her Beloved. "Until the day break and the shadows flee away I will get me to the mountain of myrrh and to the hill of frankincense." So, dear friends, the Lord "will fulfil the desire of them who fear Him" but only in Heaven shall we come to know that none of our prayers offered in faith and according to His will were denied or miscarried.

There is, however, one great danger to which we are all exposed in the matter of our prayers. It is that some sin may lurk in our heart which may grieve the Spirit of the Lord and hinder our prayers. We are, for example, commanded to live affectionately and peaceably with each other in our domestic relationships as becomes heirs together of the grace of life, "that our prayers be not hindered". An unforgiving spirit toward our fellow men–even toward those who are our enemies–may also stand as a barrier between us and the Lord. Christ warned us that God will not hear us or forgive us our trespasses unless we also forgive one another. There may be also lurking within our hearts sins like pride and covetousness; but whatever they may be, if we regard sin in our heart, the Lord will not hear us. Did not Achan's sin grieve away the Spirit of the Lord not only from himself, but also from the whole congregation of Israel? We ought always to pray that in relation to sin the Lord may bless us with more tenderness of consicience and more watchfulness in what we do, say and think. Our lapses, indeed are often grievous, but–"Who is a God like unto Thee that pardoneth iniquity and passeth by the transgression of the remnant of His heritage? He retaineth not His anger forever, because He delighteth in mercy." He is a God who is waiting to be gracious.

May the Lord give us all the grace to continue in prayer "until the day dawn and the day star arise in our hearts". "My soul waiteth for the Lord more than they that watch for the morning: I say more than they that watch for the morning". Then our Sun shall no more go down, and our prayers shall be turned into praises and our present sighs into unending songs. Happy day for all who fear and love Him! May we be of that blessed number. Amen.

THE SAINTS' HIDING PLACE

"*Be merciful to me, O God, be merciful unto me: for my soul trusteth in thee: yea, in the shadow of thy wings will I make my refuge, until these calamities be overpast*"–Psalm 57, v. 1

The earnest pleas of this Psalm emerged from the heart of David when he was in the cave of Adullam, and when Saul was seeking to take away his life. One of the mysteries of God's providence is seen in the way in which-He permits that His people, in this world, should pass through so many tribulations. They were "chosen in the furnace of affliction", and in that furnace they will remain till God's work of sanftification is perfected in their souls. But whatever 'cave' they may be in at the moment, God shall preserve them and bring them at last to see His wisdom and goodness in permitting all the sorrows which He had placed in their cup in this life.

The first thing we would notice in David's prayer is:

I. His apprehension of danger

To David his life in retrospect was a miracle of God's preserving mercy and power. There were seasons when he feared that one day he would fall into the hands of Saul. But that day never came. Although, in his own words, his enemies had almost "consumed him on the earth", he lived to see those who sought to destroy him brought to nothing. And in all his spiritual conflicts he at last overcame all his enemies by the "blood of the covenant and word of His testimony", It is a far cry from the days of David to our own times, but the same dangers are still present in our world.

God's people are conscious of the fact that they are beset by many dangers. If we bear the image of Christ in our life, and if we seek to do His will, we shall discover that our enemies are many and that their hatred toward us is unremitting. Christ warned His people against misjudging the spirit of this world. "Marvel not if the world hate you." Our enemies are not only in the world; they are also in Hell, and as we know, they are, while sin remains, within our own hearts. Beyond the shadow of Saul, David could see the more menacing shadow of Satan, who, if he could, would have swallowed him up. In comparison with the great invisible adversary "who goeth about seeking whom he may devour" our enemies of flesh and blood are weak. But these he often uses to bring God's people into distress. Men are but his tools. In all our warfare, therefore, our eyes must ever rest on Him who has all power in heaven and on earth, and who alone is able to restrain and rebuke Satan. "The Lord rebuke thee, O Satan, even the Lord who hath chosen Jerusalem rebuke thee." In His name, and employing all the weapons of our spiritual warfare, "we are more than conquerors". We have also the promise that "the God of peace shall bruise

Satan under our feet shortly". There are seasons in the life of God's people when the enemy is permitted to "come in like a flood". This happens, not only in the experience of the individual believer, but also in relation to the Church as a whole. There have been times when the Church of God has been, literally speaking, driven into the caves and dens of the earth.

Look now at:

II. His supplication for mercy

It is when we are confronted with danger and passing through great trials that we cry to God. Apart from God's mercy and sustaining grace we can do nothing. "Without me ye can do nothing." When Paul found himself buffeted by Satan he went to the Lord, praying that He might remove the thorn which Satan had so deeply buried in his flesh, if not in his spirit God's answer was—"My grace is sufficient for thee, for my strength is made perfect in weakness." It is often through the channel of our helplessness that God communicates His strength to us. In our spiritual warfare and trials the smallest degree of self-sufficiency may stand as a barrier between us and His help. And it is by the door of self-confidence that Satan often brings us low. How vividly do we see this in the case of the Apostle Peter. All might fail and deny the Lord, but not he. He in his own strength was going to follow Christ through every crisis even to death. But soon he found himself sifted in Satan's sieve. How feeble he was in the hand of the enemy of his soul the moment he forgot that only in Christ's strength could he be safe and overcome his invisible foe. Here then is David in all his conscious weakness. Through faith and prayer help came to him from above. "He shall send from heaven and save me from the reproach of him that would swallow me up. God shall send forth His mercy and His truth." As the natural creation is kept or upheld by the Word of God's power so is the spiritual. We are kept by the power of God communicated to us through God's Word. That Wod which is forever settled in the heavens is the secret of our preservation.

We notice that in his prayer David could only plead God's mercy and compassion. Although he was a subject of God's love, and a man after God's heart, and although he was highly favoured by God's choice of him as the ruler of His people, he could only pleased His mercy. God's saints in every age stand before God with their sin and undeservedness ever before them. When Paul was on the very threshold of eternal glory he could only plead the mercy of Him who came to die for sinners. "This is a faithful saying, and worthy of all acceptation, that Christ Jesus came into this world to save sinners; of whom I am chief." The sweetest drop in his cup on earth and, we believe, throughout eternity, we may discover in the words: "But I obtained mercy." "God be merciful to me a sinner" is, we think, the greatest and most appropriate prayer ever uttered by a sinful man before God. This is the prayer that is born in our hearts when first, by the work of God's Spirit within us, we see ourselves in all our misery. It is a prayer that shall remain with us until we put off this tabernacle. Throughout eternity the infinite mercy of God shall be the theme of our song. "I will sing of the mercies of the Lord for ever. For I have said, mercy shall be built up for ever." In his trial and danger David was also given a wonderful view of God's power and covenant faithfulness. Satan is described in Scripture as "the prince of the power of the air", but however high he may exalt himself in his dark designs, and in his malice to God's people, God is ever and infitely above him. He is a "power", but in comparison with the infinite power of God his power—and we speak soberly—is like that of a mere midge. It is both weak and limited. The hook of God's restraining power is ever in his jaw so that he cannot move apart from His permissive will. The floods of evil may lift up their voice:

"But yet the Lord that is on high
is more of might by far
Than noise of many waters is
or great sea billows are."

When Simon Peter saw the waves that threatened to engulf him in the storm he began to sink, but when he fastened his eyes upon Christ he was safe. The storm was changed into a calm. When, therefore, we ourselves may tremble in fear of the perils which surround us and of him who would devour us, let us lift of our eyes to our Friend and Advocate in heaven. This is the secret of our victory and peace. "He shall dwell in perfect peace whose mind is stayed on Thee, because he trusteth in Thee." Above and beyond the power of darkness is "the Most High". "There is none like unto the God of Jeshurun, who rideth upon the heaven in thy help . . . The eternal God is thy refuge and underneath are the everlasting arms." When we are therefore afraid let us realise with David that Christ has "all power" in heaven and on earth and that none ever perished who trusted in Him.

Not only did David's faith and prayer link themselves to God's power but also to His faithfulness. God has given him many promises both within the sphere of providence and of grace. He had anointed him king over Israel. He was to sit on a throne. All his enemies were to be subdued. He was to prosper in his soul and his latter end was to be like a morning without a cloud, clothed in tranquility and peace. But now he was imprisoned in a cave, a homeless wanderer, and surrounded by dark frowning providences. If there were moments in his stricken life when he let forth the cry—"Lord, where are thy former loving-kindnesses which thou swearest unto David in thy truth?" his faith was still unbroken. It was severely tried but not overcome. He knew that God would "perform all things" for him. He who, after many trials and long delays "performed the truth to Jacob and the mercy to Abraham" was his God also. His covenant with him was "ordered in all things and sure". All things were ordained to work together for his good. Dear friends, if the Lord gave us His promise He will try our faith in the promise which He gives. But in the day of adversity we must not faint. If many clouds cover our sky these will one day flee away to return no more. David knew, however, that not till his pilgrimage here would end could he be free from tribulation. This is one of God's promises to His people. But O, dear friend, how thankful we should be that in every storm there is a place of refuge.

Notice then:

III. His appreciation of shelter

He was to take refuge in the shadow of God's wings till life's storms had all passed away, or "til all these calamities be overpast". This is a figure which the Holy Spirit often uses in the Word to illustrate God's nearness to His people. It is also expressive of how God, in all His attributes, shields His people from the dangers to which they are exposed. In another Psalm he says, "Because thou hast been my help, therefore in the shadow of thy wings will I rejoice." God, in other words, is the dwelling place, or the Home, of the redeemed. "Lord," said Moses, "Thou hast been our dwelling place in all generations." From all eternity they had a place in His love and in His purpose of grace. "From everlasting to everlasting" He is their God. Under His wings the people of God are, in the words of Toplady, "as safe as those who are already in heaven". This is the great assurance given to the Church in another Psalm. "He that dwelleth in the secret place of the Most High shall abide under the shadow of the Almighty. He is my refuge and my fortress; my God, in Him will I trust." The blessing of Benjamin included this precious promise; "The beloved of the Lord shall dwell in safety by Him." When Israel of old was passing through the "great and terrible wilderness", the pillar of cloud by day and the pillar of fire by night was never withdrawn from them for a single moment. God's wings were over them. Only recently have I been thinking over the wonderful implications of the words. "Your life is hid with Christ in God." Our lives, in other words, are hid with Christ within the eternal dimensions of God's Being and love, infinitely beyond the reach and knowledge of all our enemies. From that love we can never be separated.

The word of God reveals that Christ entered our world that, through His death on the cross, He might for evermore be our hiding place. "And a man shall be an hiding place from the wind and a covert from the tempest . . . as the shadow of a great rock in a weary land." He is the cleft Rock of Ages in whom all His people find reconciliation, shelter and joy. It was "in the cleft of the Rock and in the secret places of the stair" that His Church found her refuge from the beginning of time. All who trust in Christ for salvation enjoy this great privilege of everlasting and unfailing safety. When Ruth made choice of God and His people, Boaz addressed her in these lovely words–"The Lord recompense thy work, and a full reward he given thee of the Lord God of Israel under whose wings thou art come to trust."

Truly these words speak not only of our safety and nearness to God, but also of our spiritual comfort, and of that holy communion which all who dwell in God's presence enjoy. Under His wings we have fellowship with Him and with all His people. They are our companions both in our tribulations and in our joys. They also have the same prayer, so beautifully expressed in the words:

"O, spread thy covering wings around
Till all our wanderings cease,
And at our Father's loved abode
Our souls arrive in peace."

Finally, we have here then:

IV. His anticipation of peace

"Until these calamities be overpast." David looks forward to the day when all life's storms shall be changed into a calm and when his nights of weeping shall be followed by a morning of everlasting joy. By his trials, he knows that God is preparing him for the place where, "in the great congregation" peace reigns through righteousness and where he shall sing His Redeemer's praise. His heart is already fixed, or "all set" to praise the One who has redeemed his soul, and Who had rescued him out of all his distresses. There is in every renewed heart, a longing for the perfect rest that remaineth for the people of God.

O dear friend, how difficult, and even impossible, it is to envisage the hope expressed here by David, of a state of existence without sorrow, without pain and tears, without sin and temptations or without crushing burdens. Who can envisage a world in which all who dwell love God and one another, and where there is no loneliness, fear or darkness. "For there is no night there." We know not yet what we shall be, how we shall be, or what unspeakable peace shall forever dwell within our beings in unbroken communion with the glorious Triune God. "The redeemed of the Lord shall come to Zion with songs and everlasting joy upon their heads: they shall receive joy and gladness; and sorrow and sighing shall flee away." We enter this blessed world when we draw our last breath here. "Absent from the Body", we shall be "present with the Lord". Then all our calamities shall pass away—to return no more. Death means an end and a beginning—the end of all our tribulations, and the beginning of eternal peace with God.

Dear fellow sinner, it is under His wings that Christ wants us to be. We read that in this world He wept over Jerusalem, whose inhabitants, in the presence of impending but unexpected calamities He would have gathered under His wings, but they would not. If those calamities which descended on Jerusalem in other days—because they had rejected God's Beloved Son—were sudden and terrifying, they are light compared to the storms which are about to shake our own world in these last and evil days. "For as a snare shall that day come on all them that dwell on the face of the whole earth." But these physical devastations are but the prelude to that wrath which is to come, and which, for the Christless and unrepentant shall never end. For the sinner there is no place to hide but under His wings. You who are still making light of His mercy remember that He who is now inviting you to rest in His bosom may one day meet you in judgment to dismiss you eternally from His presence. O, will you not say with David: "In the shadow of thy wings will I make my refuge." "I flee unto Thee to hide me." May God give you the wisdom and the grace to do so. Amen.

GOD'S PROMISES–OUR HERITAGE

"Whereby are given unto us exceeding great and precious promises: that by these ye might be partakers of the divine nature, having escaped the corruption that is in the world through lust"–II Peter, Ch. 1, v. 4

It is not my intention to isolate these words from their context. As the Lord will enable me, I should like to say a word not only on the promises of God, but also on the people to whom they belong, and the effect which their enjoyment or possession has on their lives in this world. Let me first offer a few remarks on:

I. The character of promises

These are here described as "exceeding great and precious". Since all these promises have their source in the sovereign love of God they are, in their very nature and value, beyond all our thoughts and limited comprehension.

God's promises are, for example, great in number. We read once of a good man who tried to count all the promises given to God's people in His Word. But no man is able to do this, since in the bosom of each promise other far reaching promises may lie, and these may be beyond our present knowledge. Is this not what the Psalmist discovered when he said: "Many are thy thoughts to us-ward: they cannot be reckoned up in order to thee: if I would declare and speak of them, they are more than can be numbered"? And in another place the Lord Himself says: "As the heavens are higher than the earth so are my thoughts higher than your thoughts."

When God commanded Abraham to look at the stars whcih graced the heavens, He told him that his seed also–the children of faith–would, like the stars remain beyond human calculation. They are a great multitude which no man can number. Only He who "counts the number of the stars" knows all those that are His. And the promises which are the heritage of Abraham's spiritual seed fall into the same limitless category.

His promises are also great in their glorious variety. We might classify God's promises in different ways. Some of them are related to His holy providence. God's providence is often "a great deep", but it brings us nothing but what He has decreed and what is in harmony with His holy permissive will. God in His Word assures His people that the ultimate end of all His dealings with them in this life is His own glory and their everlasting good.

His providence, as we know, embraces their temporal needs and their preservation in every trial. His goodness and mercy shall follow them all the days of their life. He shall not let their foot slide. He will not let them suffer beyond what they are able to endure. However hard and mysterious some of His dealings with them may be they shall at last discover how loving, how wise and faithful the Lord was in all that He allowed.

God's promises also embrace the higher spheres both of His grace and glory. Their spiritual life here is one of constant dependence on His sustaining grace. His grace is sufficient for them, and His promise is that as their day so shall their strength be. "They go from strength to strength", and each one of them, however weak or halting, shall at last appear before Him in Zion. Only in the world of glory shall all His promises have their perfect fulfilment. There we shall know how great His love was in upholding us from day to day and in supplying all our needs.

His promises also are great and precious in their value. They contain all "the unsearchable riches of Christ". "Now blessed be God who hath blessed us with all spiritual blessings in heavenly places in Christ Jesus." It was the Psalmist who said:

"They more than gold, yea, much fine gold
to be desired are."

Although David was a king, and in possession of all that this world could provide, he valued God's promises above all created things. To the true believer one promise from the lips of God is worth a million worlds, for God Himself is present in each and in all the promises that He gives. This is what lends infinite value to each one. Why did the Psalmist receive God's testimonies as his heritage for ever? Because God, the "cup of his portion", was present in His Word as the source of his eternal felicity.

"Unto me happily the lines
in pleasant places fell,
Yea, the inheritance I got
in beauty doth excel."

They are also great and precious in the absolute certainty of their fulfilment. A man may make a promise. His intentions might be honest and sincere; but through some failure, some accident, or through the arresting hand of death his promise may miscarry and come to nothing. But this cannot happen with regard to the divine promise. Every promise which God gives is united to His unfailing power and faithfulness. They are all secure within an unbroken covenant which is ordered in all things and sure. "He will perform the truth to Jacob and the mercy to Abraham." Situations, and seeming contradictions of His Word, may emerge in our life which might cause us to fear that He has forgotten to be gracious. But this cannot happen, for God has confirmed His promises to His Church by His oath. "Wherein God, willing more abundantly to shew unto the heirs of promise the immutability of His counsel, confirmed it by an oath: that by two immutable things, in which it was impossible for God to lie, we might have a strong consolation, who have fled for refuge to lay hold upon the hope set before us."

Think also of His promises *in their endless duration.* Their enjoyment shall be eternal in that kingdom which is "incorruptible and undefiled and which fadeth not away." The treasure of the saints is reserved for them in

Heaven where the thief cannot steal, and where the moth shall not corrupt. It is secure within that Word which is for ever settled in the Heavens, and which shall endure from age to age, after all created things shall have passed away. He has "magnified His word above all His name".

How unspeakably precious His promises are when we view them as the purchase of Christ's death. As our persons were bought with a price even with the precious blood of Christ, so were His promises procured for us. Not one syllable of grace and love would ever proceed from God's mouth but through the merits of His own Son with Whom alone He is well pleased. It was because Christ, "the seed of the woman", was to offer His life a ransom for many that God gave His promise of redemption and restoration to Adam, our first Covenant head. And from that solemn hour, and within an unfolding revelation of God's sovereign grace, God continued to multiply His promises till His Own eternal Son, in whom they "are all yea and amen", appeared on the scene. "Behold the Lamb of God who taketh away the sin of the world." He took our sin away that He might give us Himself. "For, He that spared not His own Son, but delivered Him up for us all, how shall He not with Him also freely give us all things?"

Let me also make brief comment on:

II. Those to whom the promises belong

They belong to all who believe. The question arises as to what constitutes true belief, or how do we become heirs of God and of His promises? The Lord Himself answers this question: "If children, then heirs, heirs of God and joint heirs with Christ." We become God's children by a new birth from Heaven, and by a gracious adoption into His family. Before we become heirs of God we must of necessity have a new nature and be established in this new and unbroken relationship with God. This process of divine grace manifested in our salvation is brought before us in the previous verse. The first emphasis, you will notice, is on the power of God. It was through the divine power that we came to know God, and to possess this heritage. The power which God exerts in the salvation of His people is exceeding great. Paul, in his prayer on behalf of the Church at Ephesus, desires that they might know "what is the exceeding greatness of His power to us-ward who believe, according to the working of His mighty power, which He wrought in Christ when He raised Him from the dead". The power which, in other words, raised up Christ from the dead is the power which gives spiritual existence to His mystical body, the Church. By nature we are dead in trespasses and in sin. We lie in a grave of sin and helplessness and misery. Only His power can save us. This power is what is behind our effectual calling–the power of the Holy Spirit. We are called out of darkness and death into light and life. We are called to glory and virtue. The ultimate end of His calling is "unto His eternal glory". We are called by Christ, to Christ and to the place where Christ dwells. "But the God of all grace who hath called us unto His eternal glory by Christ Jesus, after that ye have suffered a while, make you perfect, stablish, strengthen, settle you."

Notice also that the heirs of the promise know the Lord. It is through the knowledge of Him that they come to possess all things which pertain to life and godliness. The Spirit who quickens and calls them also enlightens their minds in the knowledge of Christ. They behold His glory as the glory of the only begotten of the Father full of grace and truth. They alone see the King in His beauty and the land of far distances. When Christ called His Bride out of her grave she was given eyes to behold Him as the "altogether lovely" One. This knowledge of Him is never given to a graceless world. Nicodemus, though a zealous churchman and morally circumspect, had no knowledge of Christ, of His kingdom or of His power, till he was born again from above. "Art thou a master in Israel and knowest not these things?" This knowledge is not perfect in this life; but "we shall know if we follow on to know the Lord". "Then shall we know even as we are known." Peter, in this Epistle, anticipated the hour when the eternal day would dawn on God's people and the day star would arise in their hearts. "The path of the just is as the shining light that shineth more and more unto the perfect day." "Light is sown unto the righteous." It is in the mirror of His Word that they see the glory of the Redeemer, and are "changed into the same image from glory to glory even as by the Spirit of the Lord". Meantime, living as we do, in a dark world and with sin casting its many shadows over our souls, His word is a lamp to our feet and a light upon our path.

With this knowledge God's children have that faith which embraces Christ in whom all the promises are given. Faith is born of need. It is an empty hand which is ever extended toward Him who is the bread of life. It is the open mouth of the soul which has the promise that God will fill it. "I opened my mouth and panted: for I longed for His commandments." Like new born babes they desire the sincere milk of the Word that they may grow thereby. There is not a promise in the Word but faith would embrace. Not only the promises which are laden with comfort, but also those which speak His just rebuke and chastisement upon as many as He loves.

Only God's people truly value His promises. Many, like Esau, may imagine that they value these until they are put to the test. Esau sold his birthright for a mess of potage. He put his temporal needs before the needs of his soul. He despised the promises because his soul was dead, and could therefore have no knowledge of, or desire for, the riches which are spiritual and eternal. There are many who have a kind of "cupboard love" to God, but when they are put to the test the mask comes off to reveal what is uppermost in their heart. They cannot say with Job "Though he slay me yet will I trust in Him", or with David, "God is all my salvation and all my desire".

Let us now look at:–

III. The effect which the promises have on their life

We notice first that because Christ dwells in the hearts of His people by faith they are made partakers of the divine nature. Not only so but the

Holy Spirit, who has made them vessels unto honour, and who applies His word to their hearts, dwells in them. "He shall abide with you for ever." The Spirit transforms them into the likeness of God. Not in this life will they attain to perfect holiness; but "He who hath begun a good work in you shall perform it until the day of Jesus Christ".

As we are told in the context it is through the indwelling of the Spirit, and through the sanctifying power of the Word that "they escape the corruption that is in the world through lust". This is what enables them to keep their garments clean in a defiled world and from having any fellowship with the unfruitfult works of darkness. They are the chaste virgins of Christ who, as their reasonable service, seek to consecrate themselves in their souls and bodies, to their Lord. In their behaviour and inward affections they seek to remain detached from a godless world. This detachment from the fashion and ways of a sinful world was the most obvious characteristic of the faith of Abraham. Abraham's faith is a pattern of the true and the living faith of all believers. When God gave him His promise, and commanded him to leave his place of abode and the people among whom he dwelt, and to go to the place which he was to possess, he immediately obeyed. From that hour he became a pilgrim and a stranger in the earth. He became a seeker of a better country. His mind, affections and desires were set on the things which are spiritual and eternal. He knew that this world with all its lusts, shadows and temptations would pass away. With the eye of faith he saw "the land of uprightness", and the glory of the One Who was to come to procure for him eternal life. "Abraham saw my day and was glad." God also gave him a foretaste of the substance of things hoped for, and told him, in many ways, that it was by faith and patience he was to obtain, in their perfect fulfilment, the promises at last.

Who can describe the joy, the consolation and the spiritual strength which God's promises impart to those who follow the Lord? Could you, dear child of God, survive even for one day without looking to Christ, the author and finisher of your faith? Ah, no. With the Psalmist you can truly say: "Unless the Lord had been my help," and "unless Thy word had been my delight, I should have perished in mine affliction". And what amid all your sorrows and trials is the source of your joy? Is it not the prospect of living with Christ in a happy eternity? And are not the sweet glimpses you get of your Beloved through the lattice of His word often like a drink from the wells of salvation to your soul? The Apostle Peter speaks of his joy of faith in his other epistle. "Whom having not seen ye love; in whom, though now ye see him not, yet believing, ye rejoice with joy unspeakable and full of glory."

Meantime let us exercise faith and patience till life's pilgrimage is over; and "let us not be weary in well doing, for in due season we shall reap if we faint not". Let us remember His other exhortation and promise: "Wherefore beloved, seeing that ye look for such things be diligent that ye may be found of Him in peace, without spot and blameless."

My friends, have you made a personal discovery of the value of God's

Word, of His promises, of the Gospel which is "glad tidings of great joy"? And do you, in the words of David, rejoice in His word "as those who find great spoil"? Can you say to Christ, or have you already said it, "To whom shall we go but unto Thee for thou hast the words of eternal life?" Do you know the joy of those who have found in His word "the pearl of great price" and in whose heart His love dwells? Is His word to you "better than thousands of gold and silver"? Happy are you if this is true of you. O that Mary's portion–the good part that shall never be taken from us–may be ours also. Amen.

THE ETERNAL CITY

"For here have we no continuing city, but we seek one to come."–Hebrews, Ch. 13, v. 14)

These words speak of two cities, one of which belongs to the order of time and the other to the eternal world. The one is earthly and is therefore going to pass away. The other is heavenly and therefore permanent. For our edification let us just consider:

I. The city which cannot endure

"Here we have no continuing city."

There is nothing more obvious than that change is written over all things which pertain to this life. There are things which fade away before our eyes. "The grass withereth, and the flower thereof falleth away; but the word of the Lord endureth for ever." We may sometimes stand by a meadow and see the lovely and varied flowers which blossom under the summer sun. Then we return before the autumn end to find that they have all faded away. Their momentary appearance is a true symbol of man's life in this world. "The voice said, Cry. And he said, what shall I cry? All flesh is grass, and all the goodliness thereof is as the flower of the field . . . because the spirit of the Lord bloweth upon it; surely the people is grass." "We do all fade as a leaf." The Lord in His word reminds us that our life here is "a vapour which appeareth for a little while and then vanisheth away".

"For over it the wind doth pass,
and it away is gone.
And of the place where once it was
it shall no more be known."

Let us walk for a brief hour along the path of memory and recall those who once inhabited our different communities. Many of them have vanished from the scene. Or we can look around us in the church where we worship to see how many of our beloved friends are no longer there. We are all moving in the same vast procession toward the grave and toward eternity. Some of us get many reminders in ourselves that here we have no continuing city. Our step may be slower, our eye may be dimmer than they once were. We can say with another:

"My wonted strength and force He hath
abated in the way."

Not only is this true of human life, but even the cities of this world, however impressive they may appear over many centuries of time, are all destined to pass away. The page of history tells us of empires, nations and cities which have long since passed into oblivion. Some of these have, for their evil ways, been harried out of existence by the righteous judgments of God.

Even the things which appear to be permanent shall one day pass away. Not only is our own world to pass away, but also the mysterious and awesome universe by which we are on this tiny planet surrounded. When you stand at your door at night and look toward the sky with its countless lovely and silent orbs, you are looking at the same stars which Adam and Eve saw in Paradise. These are the same which Abraham also saw when the Lord, in His Covenant promise, said to him: "Look now toward Heaven and tell the stars if thou be able to number them:" and He said unto him, "so shall thy seed be." These were the heavens which David saw when inspired of the Spirit of God he sang:

"The heavens God's glory do declare
the skies His hand works preach:
Day utters speech to day, and night
to night doth knowledge teach."

While His works of creation and providence reveal God's eternal power and Godhead what, on the other hand, is His own witness in relation to these? Here it is: "And, Thou, Lord, in the beginning hast laid the foundation of the earth: and the heavens are the works of thine hands; they shall perish but thout remainest; and they all shall wax old as doth a garment; and as a vesture shalt thou fold them up, and they shall be changed; but thou art the same, and thy years shall not fail." "Lift up your eyes to the heavens, and look upon the earth beneath: for the heavens shall vanish away like smoke, and the earth shall wax old like a garment . . . but my salvation shall be for ever, and my righteousness shall not be abolished."

Once, and whilst I was still a young man, I listened to an eminent servant of Christ as he preached a remarkable sermon on the eternity of our glorious Redeemer and the transitoriness of all created things. "This was He," he said, "Who stood by the cradle of the universe when it was born, and this is He Who shall stand by its bier when it shall finally pass away." "The world passeth away and the lusts thereof," but Jesus Christ is "the same yesterday, and today, and for ever".

But a question which we must ask is, Does man come within this category? Does he also go out of existence and cease to be? No; man is an eternal being. We know that our life here is but for a moment, but our physical death, or our departure from this world, marks the beginning of an endless existence either in a state of unspeakable happiness with God or of misery without Him. And so as a mark of God's people and for their comfort the Apostle speaks of another city:

II. The city which is permanent or eternal

Many glorious things may be said of this city. "Glorious things are spoken of thee, O city of God." One of the most glorious things that may be said of it is that God Himself is its Builder and Maker. Earthly cities are built by poor fallible men, and the many defects which characterise their own minds are also seen in the works of their hands. But the glorious Lord

Who laid the foundations of this city and its spiritual temple shall bring it into a state of eternal perfection. "He shall bring forth the headstone thereof with shoutings, crying, Grace, grace unto it." All the hosts of heaven, both angels and men, cannot but adore this lovely work of God.

When the Scripture speaks of Heaven as a city that has foundations the meaning is that it is immovable and outwith the categories of space and time, and forever beyond the destructive and contaminating influence of sin. It is incorruptible and undefiled, and shall never fade away. It is the city of the Great King Who is infinitely holy and whose place of abode is eternally holy also. "There shall in no wise enter into it anything that defileth, neither whatsoever worketh abomination or maketh a lie." Evil, in the words of the Psalm, shall "never dwell" in God's presence: not even the smallest shadow of it. When eveil invaded the lives of those angels who kept not their first estate they were instantly banished into the outer darkness. But this cannot recur, since all elect angels and men are eternally secure within the everlasting and unchangeable rightesousness of Christ.

This is also a city prepared for the redeemed by Him Who loved them. In this world many words of unspeakable consolation dropped from His lips. Among these were the words: "Let not your hearts be troubled; ye believe in God, believe also in me. In my Father's house are many mansions; if it were not so, I would have told you. I go to prepare a place for you . . . that where I am, there ye may be also." "Father, I will that they also whom Thou hast given me be with me where I am."

Although this city was prepared by God for all the heirs of salvation before the foundation of the world, there is a sense in which it was also prepared for them by their Redeemer. It was His death that purchased it for them. Heaven, as the Apostle tells us elsewhere, is a "purchased possession". It was He who opened its doors for all His people to enter in. "I am the door." He alone is the way into God's presence. Besides, all the blessings which shall enrich and rejoice His people for ever were procured for us by His merits and death. The rich feast laid on His table in the glorious upper sanctuary He also purchased by His death. It is a place made fragrant by His all-prevailing intercession and also blessed and warmed by that love which passeth knowledge.

Although Heaven, or this city, is a place, heaven is essentially and supremely the everlasting enjoyment of, or our indwelling in, God. "Lord," said Moses, "Thou hast been our dwelling place in all generations." To dwell with God and in God is the deepest and most ravishing desire of all His people. "My soul thirsteth for God, for the living God: when shall I come and appear before God?" (Psalm 42.) On earth He is often a "little sanctuary" to them. Jacob spoke of Bethel as God's house. Literally speaking there was no house there: only God Himself–The One whose tabernacle is with men.

And, O, how intimate are the relationship and communion within this city or Home. On earth our Lord spoke of His Father and our Father. The prayer which, by His Spirit, He sealed on their hearts began with these words: "Our Father which art in Heaven." Christ Himself is the husband of His Church. "Thy Maker is thine husband; The Lord of hosts is His name." "He that hath the bride is the Bridgegroom." All the inhabitants of this city also belong to the same spiritual family. The ties which unite them together are more intimate, more tender and nearer than the natural ties which bind us to our closest earthly relatives and friends. And these can never be dissolved. All the members of Christ's mystical body are eternally united to one another in love and in their glorious Head.

The many mansions which make up this city are all occupied. Love, holiness and unbroken peace fill the hearts of those who dwell there. Perfect recognition of, and full communion with, one another in the Lord shall be part of their joy. In this city they shall all meet to part no more. There, their joy and communion with God and with one another shall be full.

How easy it is for those who truly seek this city to discover that they are unwanted strangers in this cold world! Many of them live in communities where their ways, their Christian witness and their separation from the unfruitful works of darkness, as well as from false teachings and unscriptural forms of worship, offend the ungodly and the blind. In the Book of Malachi we read of those who, like the few names in Sardis, maintained their holy unity and love in the Truth, and who refused to defile their lives in any active association with a graceless world. But not till they come to the Jerusalem which is from above shall their loneliness and all that grieves them here pass away. There Ruth and Naomi shall weep no more. There David and Jonathan shall never bid each other a sad farewell. There your own tears over the departure of your loved ones in the Lord shall be wiped from your eyes. There the Birde shall never mourn with those words on her lips: "Saw ye Him whom my soul loveth?" "But I will see you again and your heart shall rejoice and your joy no man shall taketh from you."

This city is also a place of everlasting rest. "There remaineth, therefore, a rest to the people of God." There is a real sense in which God's people enter into rest even in this troubled life. "We who have believed do enter into rest." This is a rest which has its souce in a covenant relationship and union with Christ as our Saviour, in the removal and forgiveness of all our sins through His death, and in our obedience to his Word which says: "Come unto me all ye that labour and are heavy laden and I will give you rest." Those who have come to Him have found their place of rest, in His bosom and love.

Not long ago I read a sermon by the excellent "Archie" Cook on "God's Unspeakable Gift". At the end of his discourse he dwelt on the words of Sephaniah: "And he shall rest in His love." The good man reminds us that in the salvation of His people all the attributes of God rested eternally in the finished work of His beloved Son. There, in the words of the Psalm they "kiss each other". Behind God's unspeakable gift of His own Son lies the infinite, the fathomless and unchangeable love of the Triune God. In that love He shall for ever rest and rejoice with singing over His people. "This is my rest for ever: here will I dwell; for I have desired it."

This is the love in which those who love Him also rest. John, "the disciple whom Jesus loved", and who so deeply loved His Lord, rested on His bosom. Mary rested at the feet of her Lord, drinking inthe words of everlasting life. The Church in communion with her Beloved would have no one disturb her peace. "I charge you, O ye daughters of Jerusalem that ye stir not up, nor awake my love, till He please." O, how in times of restlessness and distraction we should, like the Psalmist, address our soul: "Return unto this rest, O my soul, for the Lord hath dealt bountifully with thee." "He maketh me to lie does in green pastures." "As the herd goeth down into the valley, so the Spirit of the Lord caused him to rest." Such words as these speak of those blessed foretastes of that rest awaiting them in the heavenly City.

But the life of God's people here is also a warfare. Their conflicts and sufferings continue with them till they are beyond the reach of sin, Satan and all the snares of an evil world. But, dear suffering friend, listen to His words: "O thou afflicted, tossed with the tempest and not comforted, behold, I will lay thy stones with fair colours, and lay thy foundations with sapphires." "And all thy children shall be taught of the Lord and great shall be the peace of thy children."'

This city is also a place of inconceivable loveliness–a loveliness which is all derived from the One who is in Himself "altogether lovely". Christ, Who is the Sun of righteousness and the bright and morning Star shall communicate His own beauty and image both to the place of His abode and to the people who dwell therein. God, in the person of the Father, is also the Father of lights with whom there is no variableness neither shadow of turning. The Son, Who is eternally in His bosom, is the brightness of His glory and the express image of His person. And the equal glory of the Holy Spirit shall be for ever reflected in the perfect sanctification of the Church. For ever she shall look forth as the morning and be clothed with the sun that shall no more go down. "And they that be wise shall shine as the brightness of the firmament, and they that turn many to righteousness as the stars for ever and ever." Adding to the loveliness of this place is the River of Life and the Tree of Life which shall for ever satisfy and delight all who dwell therein. Our well springs shall be all in God. In adding to the loveliness of this city, and above the Throne on which the Lamb sits, is the rainbow "in sight like unto an emerald". This shall be the lovely emblem of that covenant which is "ordered in all things and sure", and over which no cloud shall ever pass. It shall be an everlasting reminder that our security and happiness wholly rest in Him who is, "The Lord, our Righteousness".

There also we shall walk on golden streets. He who passed through a vale of tears, and whose feet were nailed to the cross of shame has paved these with His love.

This city is also a place of praise. Even in this world is there anything more affecting thean to hear God's praise being sung by His people in the public means of grace, especially when His presence is among them? During the great evangelical revival in Scotland, Wales and England those multitudes who would gather together to worship God often felt as they were singing His praise as if they were already in the vestibule of Heaven. Often they felt their hearts melting as they sang such words as these:

"Praise waits for thee in Sion, Lord;
to thee vows paid shall be.
O thou that hearer art of prayer
all flesh shall come to thee."

"Within the congregation great
my praise shall be of thee:
My vows before them that him fear
shall be performed by me."

or the words:

"When God the people writes, he'll count
that this man born was there.
There be that sing and play: and all
my well-springs in thee are." (Psalm 87)

But infinitely sweeter shall our songs be in the city above, when our "poor lisping stammering tongues "shall be transformed into instruments of perfect praise of Him Who loved us and whom we shall love for ever and ever.

Let me now end with a brief commen on:

III. Those who are seeking this city

Living, as we do, in an atheistic and materialistic age there are many millions of the human race who refuse to believe that there is a spiritual, supernatural world. To them there is no God. Man is but a rational animal with no life beyond the grave. Heaven is but an empty dream, a species of wishful thinking. Other millions there are who believe that man is a spiritual being, but are ensnared by cults, false idolatrous religions, and many other dangerous delusions. And there are, sad to say, those who may give a formal assent to the doctrines of Scripture on this solemn theme, but whose lives answer not to the description which God gives of His people in His Word. And there are others who, like Balaam, would die the death of the righteous but would not live their life. Like him they would go to Heaven while they still walk on the broad way which leads to destruction. But those who are truly seekers of this city are a "peculiar people" who bear marks of which a godless world is ignorant and to which they are often hostile.

They are, in a word, a people whom God, by His Spirit, has convinced that they have immortal souls, and that they are by nature lost–"without God and without hope in the world". He has convinced them that there is no escaping that death which is the wages of sin apart from God's grace. They stand before Him under the just sentence of death, conscious that all their own righteousnesses are but "filthy rags". Their prayer is: "God be merciful to me a sinner."

But God exercises his mercy and power in their salvation. He makes them "a willing people in a day of His power". He gives him a new heart. They become new creatures in Christ. They enter, spiritually speaking, a new world, which by faith they see as in a glass. Their affections and desires are set on the things which are above.

These people walk in the new and living way which leads to the city of God. "And an highway shall be there and a way, and it shall be called the way of holiness: the unclean shall not pass over it: but it shall be for those: the wayfaring men, though fools, shall not err therein." "Who is wise, and he shall understand these things? prudent, and he shall know them? for the ways of the Lord are right, and the just shall walk in them: but the transgressors shall fall therein."

"Them also in a way to walk
that right is he did guide,
That they might to a city go,
wherein they might abide."

They persevere inthe way of obedience to God's Word. "This is the way, walk ye in it." And all the saints from the beginning of time have had David's prayer in their heart and on their lips:

"In thy law's paths make me to go,
for I delight therein."

The implications of such a prayer is that they have left the ways of a godless world, however fair and deceptive in some instances such ways may be. They have made the discovery that there is but one "narrow way" that leads to life and which, comparatively speaking, only a few shall find.

One evidence of our being in God's way is that God Himself is our Companion in the way, and that we enjoy sweet foretastes of the pleasures which are reserved for us at God's right hand. Many years ago I conducted a service in the Outer Isles at which the excellent "Happy Norman"—as he was known— was present. That morning I made a comment about Abraham being in the land of promise while he had it only in the promise; and that God's people had their days in Heaven while they were still on earth, or while they had Heaven but in the promise. I could see that the dear man was deeply affected by my remark, for it was truly expressive of his own holy spiritual walk in this world.

In the Epistle to the Hebrews the Apostle speaks of the present great privilege and standing of God's people in their covenant Head. "But ye are come unto Mount Sion, and unto the city of the living God, the heavenly Jerusalem, and to an innumerable company of angels, to the general assembly and church of the first born, which are written in Heaven, and to God the Judge of all, and to the spirits of just man made perfect."

Friend, do you walk in the way of the Lord? If not, remember that there is no neutral ground and that here you have no continuing city. Your time is short. God speaks to you. "Turn ye, turn ye, why should you die." May the Lord give you the will and the grace to embrace Jesus Christ as he is freely offered to you in the Gospel. And if you do, we shall one day meet in that glorious place which Christ is preparing for all who love Him and where our praises shall be of Him who loved us and gave Himself for us.

THE GREAT CHALLENGE

"Bring ye all the tithes into the storehouse, that there may be meat in My house, and prove Me now herewith, saith the Lord of hosts, if I will not open you the windows of heaven, and pour you out a blessing, that there shall not be room enough to receive it." –(Mal. Ch. 3, v. 10)

It was a law in ancient Israel that a man should give a tenth of his substance to the cause of God; and although there is no specific enforcement of this rule under the Gospel dispensation we are not to infer that Christians should give less toward the service of God than they did in Israel in ancient times. God, has indeed, given us immeasurably more than He had given to them and, therefore, our practical appreciation of His grace and spiritual blessings hould be all the greater.

What has God given us which He had not given to them? Let me tell you by quoting two verses from the New Testatement: "He that spared not His own Son, but delivered Him up for us all, how shall He not with Him also freely give us all things?" "For ye know the grace of our Lord Jesus Christ that though He was rich yet for our sakes He became poor that ye through His poverty might be rich." Israel of old were living in expectation of the coming of the Just One in whom all the promised blessings of the Old Testament were to be fulfilled. We live in the Gospel age of greater fulness and revelation, when all the purchased gifts of redemption are now available to "whosoever will". In the light of all this, how much more do we owe Him!

In that far off age men robbed God of His lawful offerings. This brought a blight on all their temporal prosperity. But a greater calamity was that the Heavens were sealed and that no spiritural blessing refreshed the spirit of the people. There are also many in this age of material prosperity whose hands and givings are "withered" in relation to God's cause. They have ample for themselves but little or nothing for the maintenance of God's cause in the world. And because of this God, as in the case of Israel, may dry up the wells of their temporal favour also.

The renewal of God's favour to Israel was conditional on the fulfilling, on their part, of their several obligations to the Holy One. So the Lord presented them with:

I. A great challenge

"Prove me now." In giving these words a spiritual application one could say that there is today among many of the Lord's people a yearning for a genuine spiritual revival. We seem to be helpless in the presence of the prevailing evils which surround us on all sides, and we know that without His help we can do nothing. "Salvation is of the Lord." We live in times of unparalleled danger, and only an outpouring of the Holy Ghost can prevent a greater onrush of evil sweeping over the world. What is it that prevents the blessing? The enemy is come in like a flood and only the Spirit of the Lord can arrest his power. Does not this prophecy provide us with an answer which is a relevant to us today as it was to that age?

In the context we read of how the Lord revealed the many dark obstructions in the way of a blessing. But the people, generally, were quite unconscious of their sin. Therefore we get a presumptuous reiteration of questions which they fling in the very face of God. "Wherein have we robbed thee?" "Wherein shall we return?" "What have we spoken so much against thee?" This arrogant disavowal of sin was the measure of their spiritual hardness, decline and blindness. And before He would bless them they would need to rend their hearts, to mend their ways and to examine their lives.

We, also, must learn the hard lesson that the way to a blessing is by a discovery of our own trangressions, by personal repentance and by a deeper and more genuine consecration of ourselves to God. Only in the garments of repentance, of humility and self abasement, and by retracing our steps in the path of new obedience, will God meet us in the words– "Prove me *now*".

They were to prove Him in His infinite mercy. Their sins were great, but God's mercy in Christ is like a great deep which could cover them all. In His beloved Son He is a God merciful and gracious. His mercy in Christ is the foundation of our everlasting security. It endures because God endures. "For I am the Lord, I change not. therefore ye sons of Jacob are not consumed."

They were to prove Him in His promises. The Bible is teeming with promises related to the welfare and revival of the Church of God. All the promises are the heritage of believers, and they should plead their fulfilment at the Throne of Grace. How can we prosper if this great duty is neglected? Is it true of us what was true of Israel in other days? "There is none that calleth upon Thy Name, that stirreth up himself to take hold of Thee; for Thou hast hid Thy face from us."

God was to be proved also in His saving power. The history of the Church of Christ is replete with impressive instances of His gracious and timely intervention in answer to prayer. Think of Israel in Egypt surrounded by the powers of darkness, and God leading them forth by a strong and outstretched arm! This great and solemn event in the history of the church and of the ancient world was an answer to prayer. God said to Moses: "Surely I have seen the affliction of My people which are in Egypt and I have heard their cry and I am come down to save them." Think of Babylon with its giant walls broken in an instant by the finger of Jehovah. Out of that "grave" and place of despair the Lord led His people. It was an answer to prayer. For many years the Lord's people in Europe had been praying for the spiritual revival of the Church of God and for the destruction of the papal power which held the nations in its grasp. Then the sound of a hammer was heard nailing God's answer to the door of a church in Wittenburg. The Reformation was on the way. God opened the windows of heaven, and there was the sound of an abundance of rain. Nations were born in a day. Truly, this also was an answer to prayer.

The people to whom God immediately addressed this challenge did not prove Him. They slept on. They sinned on. They retained their silence. What was His answer to this? Here it is. "I shall yet be enquired of by the house of Israel." And it may also happen that the children who are now born into the world will wrestle for the blessing for which we fail to plead and which we so lightly esteem.

"Prove me *now*." The present hour is ours. Some Christians are always thinking of the future; and others seem to live in the past. "Now" is God's Word. Now is our time. All the spiritual resources of our Lord are now at our disposal if we ask in faith.

Think then of:

II. God's great promise

In the Gospels we read that before God rent the heavens and came down in the person of His own dear Son there were those within His church who prayerfully waited for "the consolation of Israel." We could mention such saints as Simeon and Anna. Although Christ came into the world at the moment forordained from everlasting, yet His coming was an answer to prayer! Throughout the centuries of the twilight dispensation of the law, God had a people who waited for the coming of the Lord Jesus. The church in the exercise of faith, patience and prayer was waiting for her Beloved. "Until the day break and the shadows flee away, turn my beloved and be thou like a roe or a young hart on the amountains of Bether." Then suddenly in one glad hour—an hour laden with a blissful destiny for millions of souls—the door of Heaven opened and Christ appeared. "Lo, I come! In the colume of the Book it is written of me." This was how God honoured His promise and answered the prayers of His people.

Before our Lord ascended up into Heaven He commanded His followers to wait for the promise of the Father. In that unknown upper room in Jerusalem a few Christians were on their knees waiting for the promised outpouring of the Holy Ghost. God was to open the windows of Heaven and pour them out a blessing. In God's unalterable order their prayers were linked to the promise. And in one wonderful hour the windows of Heaven were opened and God rained down on the world a blessing, the far-reaching effects of which we cannot grasp in time. It was such an abundant blessing that the infant Church proved too small a vessel to contain it. The life-giving streams flowed to the ends of the earth. Weary continents and nations were raised from spiritual death and moral degradation into a new sphere of power and life. Men bearing "Good News from a far country" brought the word of salvation to people and lands where the Lord was unknown. And through the intervening centuries the Lord continued, in answer to the prayers of His people, to revive and enlarge His church. It was on a wave of spiritual power that the Reformed Church was born.

Europe and America, along with this favoured island, were saved from the tyranny and perversions of the Roman anti-Christ. Britain enjoyed such a rich measure of this blessing as brought spiritual healing to other lands. Thousands of men and women dedicated to God's service left our shores to tell hitherto inaccessible peoples of God's redeeming love in Christ. Our Bible Societies sent the Gospel in their own tongue to millions of men. "Great was the company of them that published it."

Today we are living in a strange and confused world. Terrifying events, emerging in quick succession, are throwing mankind into anxious situations. In our own nation the process of moral degeneration and spiritual apostasy is deepening very rapidly. Without exaggeration the present governments have done more in the last decade to destroy our moral foundations than other governments have done in the last three hundred years. Is there any hope for us? No; none without the intervention and the saving power of God. He alone is the God of salvation. His saving power is still available. Do we pray for this? If not, there may be only one alternative. Instead of a blessing the heavens may again rain destruction upon the nations of the earth. Some of us believe that this is now inevitable—that we have reached the point of no return. In the following chapter (Mal. Ch. 4, v. 1) we read of "the day that shall burn as an oven" when the wicked and the proud shall be as stubble. The ominous shadow of nuclear devastation is over our world. If the deep anxieties of the times fail to send us to our knees in prayer, what will?

Allow me to give these words another and a nearer application. We have all read and heard of the mighty works done in these parts in other days—days when the windows of Heaven were truly opened and when, through God's blessing, a rich spiritual harvest was reaped and gathered to God. Men and women were, in those days, wrestling with God that He would refresh and gladden His heritage by pouring out His blessing. And the Holy Spirit did work among the people. When we read of God's mighty works in the days of John Kennedy, John MacDonald, Hector MacPhail and "Big MacRae" we can hardly believe that we inhabit the same place. What would happen if, literally speaking, no shower of rain fell upon us in over a hundred years? No man or beast could survive such a calamity. But a greater disaster than this has come upon us in that the Lord has sealed the heavens, and the prayers of the remnant which remain and who think upon His name are still unanswered. Why is the Lord a stranger in the land? There is only one answer to this question. Our sin and our silences are the cause of our leanness and deprivation. An old Christian man in Ross-shire used to tell of how in the days of his youth—both before and after the Sabbath services—one could overhear, in the vicinity of a certain church, the subdued voices of many men and women in prayer behind hedges and trees. They were praying that God's presence and power might accompany the preaching of the Word and that sinners might be converted to God. In those days "the voice of the turtle was still heard in our land". It was "the Day Spring from on High". One who recently attended meetings of prayer in that very place saw only two men present. Afterwards at the funeral of an earthbound farmer, over a hundred stood by the grave. The dead are there burying their dead. As he stood there he could not but recall the words: "To these long desolations Thy feet lift do not tarry."

Is it not also true that a spirit of worldliness has robbed us of God's presence? We became preoccupied, beyond all that is wise, with our earthly concerns. Like Jeshurun of old many have "waxed fat and kicked". In the measure in which we have propsered in material things, in the same measure have we undergone a tragic decline in our spiritual state. Our sins of omission and commission have, like foxes, or like the boar out of the forest, played havoc with the vine of true godliness in our midst. Nor is this decline confined to any one place. It is general throughout the land. We see not our signs, and we can only mourn over the years which the locusts have eaten.

Many of God's people have discovered that it is easy to alienate and grieve the Spirit of the Lord from their midst; but it is not so easy to get Him back again. This is the greatest judgment which can possibly come upon us in this life. A cloud of thick darkness is over many places where once the Lord dwelt and where His Name was great. Many are unaware of what has happened and unconcerned over this loss and decline. "Wherein," they also say, "have we sinned against Thee?" Some have, like those of old, kept His ordinances, retained their religious formality and put on a serious face. But before we can have a Bethel we must first have a Bochim. Before we can look for His blessing we must rend our hearts, confess our sins and those of our fathers and show a great and more serious interest in His cause. We must retrace our steps back into the path of repentance, prayer, and a holy humility before the Lord. We must prove that we love Him by our practical interest in His word, His Day and the needs of His Kingdom in the world. These are some of the spiritual "tithes" which He demands before the windows of Heaven open in mercy. Are you offended at what I say? Beware. We are in God's presence and to Him we must give an account.

The last word I would say is this—before we can truly give anything to the Lord with which He may be pleased we must first of all give Him ourselves. He wants our hearts in a personal obedience to His Word. Come to Him as you are—a poor lost sinner. His promise is that if we do He shall in no wise cast us out. How did the poor prodigal rejoice the heart of his father when he retraced his steps to his door! Christ wants us as we are that He might make us what we are not—new and holy creatures in Himself. He came to seek and to save that which was lost. If we give Him not our hearts we give Him nothing.

May He bless His Word.

"WHAT MIGHT HAVE BEEN"

"O, that thou hadst hearkened to My commandments! Then had thy peace been as a river, and they righteousness as the waves of the sea." —Isaiah Ch. 48, v. 18)

If each of us sat down to write the story of our past lives we might write a chapter on—"What Might Have Been". But this we would wisely refrain from doing. Each of us knows that life in retrospect has many regrets which lie concealed within our own hearts and memories. However brief and circumspect our pilgrimage here may be we all have sad recollections of things done or left undone. This is true especially of God's people. They know the multitude of ways in which they come short of the glory of Him whom they would have more devotedly loved and served. The Lord in His Word tells us of the perfect peace of those whose minds are stayed on Him; but because our minds are too often distracted and set on "things seen" we deprive ourselves of this peace which comes through daily communion with God and acquiescence in His will.

But the words of our text primarily refer to Israel whom God had so greatly honoured in embracing as His own people. "Ye only have I known of all the families of the earth." There is nothing in history more tragic or more sad than the repeated rejection by Israel of their God, and their persistent refusal to hearken to His Commandments. His many appeals to them throughout centuries of time, both to love Him and to obey His Word, ended in their crucifying the promised Messiah, the Eternal I AM—the incarnate and personal word who entered our world to save the lost. It was He who wept over them in this world. "How often would I have gathered thy children together, even as a hen gathereth her chickens under her wings, but we would not."

But all humanity is involved in this great disaster and guilty of this rebellion against God. God created man in righteousness and holiness. The supreme end set before him was to glorify God and enjoy Him for ever. While man remained in a state of righteousness and obedience to His Will, peace filled his heart. Now in his fallen state and ruined by sin, he cannot, rest. The confused, lawless and evil world in which we dwell is but a mild reflection of man's heart which, apart from the regenerating power of God's Spirit, is "desperately wicked". God, however, is still speaking to us in mercy, and reassuring us that if we return to Him and obey Him, He will bless us with eternal peace.

In meditating on these precious words, let us make a comment first on:

I. The source of this peace

Literally speaking all rivers may be traced to their own sources; but this river of God's peace has only one ultimate source. It is that sovereign purpose and eternal love of God which shall for ever remain bevond our knowledge. It "passeth knowledge." This was something within the Being of God before His chosen people came into existence, and it shall remain within His being for ever. "Godis love." He is "Jehovah Shalom"–the God of Peace. Whatever exercise God may give His wrath in the destruction of those who continue to oppose His Will, He, the God of Peace, shall, in relation to His people, remain the same "yesterday, today and forever.". This peace He will communicate in its fulness to all His people in that glorious world where nothing shall ever disturb it. "There remaineth therefore a rest to the people of God." But since this theme is something which lies beyond the comprehension of men and angels we move on to our second thought which is:

II. The channel through which this peace flows

As God is the source of this peace He is also the channel through which it flows. Christ, the second Person in the glorious Trinity, is the only mediator between God and man. One of the reasons why He entered our fallen world in our nature and in a state of humiliation was that He might restore that which He took not away. "And a man shall be as an hiding place from the wind, and a covert from the tempest, and as rivers of water in a dry place." When, through our fall, sin took possession of our beings all peace left us. He alone could restore that peace to our souls again. The terrifying restlessness, which is a permanent characteristic of fallen humanity, has its source in our spiritual ignorance of God and His way. "The way of peace have they not known." As we can have no inward peace, or true peace with one another, we can have no peace with God but through our Lord Jesus Christ. He alone is our peace. He is the Prince of Peace. Through His merits and death He procured peace for all who believe in His Name. When, for example, the high priest on the great day of atonement entered into the most holy place with the blood of the covenant, the awesome, benign and holy presence of Him who dwelt between the Cherubims was the evidence that peace was, typically, established between Him and His people. When Christ entered Heaven as our Surety, and as the One who had, on behalf of His people, satisfied and exalted God's law and justice, eternal peace was procured and for ever established between God and all for whom He died. "For thus saith the Lord, Behold I will extend peace to her like a river." In the saving of the Church the attributes of God rest in His work and love. Here also the awakened soul finds rest, and the stricken conscience, which has been oppressed by a burden of guilt, enters into peace with God through that blood "which speaketh better things than that of Abel." An old man who had entered into this soul-rest once remarked that his conscience which had for many days suffered the pangs of guilt could now sing as if he had never sinned. But here we must emphasise that this peace "reigns through righteousness". Thy righteousness shall be as "the waves of the sea"–pure, active and everlasting.

The waves here spoken of are not the noisy broken waves which may dash on unclean shores. In another chapter the prophet speaks of the wicked who are like the troubled sea which cannot rest and whose waters cast up mire and dirt. Their nature, their associations and ways are wholly corrupt. What they consider to be their best are often their worst; for by nature "all our righteousnesses are as filthy rags". The sea here referred to is the sea of God's infinite holiness, justice and love. The righteousness of all who are accepted in Christ remains for ever spotless and perfect. It is as unchangeable as God Himself. As the Psalmist tells us it endures for ever. Therefore, those who stand in it can never fall.

Is there any doctrine in God's Word that brings greater comfort to the soul than that Christ is our Righteousness? "The Lord our Righteousness" is the foundation of our peace and all the blessings of the covenant of grace. His righteousness like a pure ocean of infinite depth has covered all our sins for ever. To Him all our sins were imputed. He bore them in His own body on the Tree. He removed them from our persons for ever "as far as the east is distant from the west". They are for ever put behind His back and out of His sight. He shall remember them no more. And as our sins were imputed to Him, His perfect righteousness is imputed to all who, by faith, rest on His merits. We are complete in Him. We are accepted in the Beloved. God is well pleased with Him, and He is well pleased with all who are adorned in the best robe of His righteousness. In Christ He sees no iniquity in His Jacob or perverseness in His Israel.

R.M. McCheyne, in his famous hymn, speaks of the hour when he found peace in the "Lord our Righteousness":

"My terrors all vanished before that sweet name;
My guilty fears banished, with boldness I came
To drink at the fountain, life-giving and free—
Jehovah Tsidkenu is all things to me."

"There is therefore *now* no condemnation to them which are in Christ Jesus." In the day of our Justification by faith in Christ, God's Law and Justice led us out of our bondage for ever to enjoy the glorious liberty of the people of God. The day of our justification marks the beginning of that peace of which Christ spoke in this world. "Peace I leave with you, My peace I give unto you: not as the world giveth, give I unto you. Let not your heart be troubled, neither let it be afraid." This is the peace that keeps, or garrisons, our hearts and minds. "And the work of righteousness shall be peace; and the effect of righteousness quietness and assurance for ever."

The Holy Spirit is another supreme means through which this peace flows into our soul. By Him we are regenerated and given an imparted righteousness. The promises of the Gospel He applies to our souls. It is He who makes us willing in a day of His power and, in the words of the Psalm, to "hear what God the Lord will speak: for He will speak peace unto His people and to His saints." But before this peace lodged in our hearts He had to awaken us out of our own deceptive peace. From the mountain which cannot be touched we heard the threatenings of His law: "Cursed is every one that continueth not in all things which are written in the book of the law to do them." With Moses, and many others since his day, we could say, "I exceedingly fear and tremble". By that word we discovered that we were under the just sentence of death, and this sentence we found within ourselves. But the time came when in mercy the Lord passed us and said, "*Live*", and when He made our time a time of love. By His Word He stilled the storm. "Peace be still. And there was a great calm." Our souls found rest in the clefts of the Rock of Ages. Like the dove which had left t the ark and which found no resting place outwith it, the soul of man can only have rest in Christ. "I will give you rest." When God spoke the word of reconciliation to our hearts we could then say: "Return unto thy rest, O my sould; for the Lord hath dealt bountifully with thee." Faith in Christ and in His Word is the secret of spiritual peace. "Great peace have they that love Thy law, and nothing shall offend them." Yes, dear friend, peace comes through His Word. Although you love the whole of God's Word perhaps there is a verse or a promise in the Bible which is particularly precious to you, for it was through that word that you first entered into soul-rest in God.

How wonderful it is also to know that the blessed Spirit is He who shall abide with us for ever. We become His temple. Whatever our struggles with the corruption of our nature, our souls are now occupied by the Holy Dove. In the barren spiritual wilderness, where the dragon lay, He now dwells, causing it to blossom as the rose. By His holy presence within us He shall at last bring to perfection His work of sanctification. How great must the love of the Spirit be when He would dwell within sinful creatures and O, how careful we should be not to grieve Him by our sins. God's exhortation to all His people is: "Be ye holy, for I am holy."

Let me now say a word on:

III. The blessings which this peace brings to those who enjoy it

The figure which the Spirit uses in our text to describe this peace is full of meaning. Literally speaking, the rivers which flow through our world bring many blessings to men. They are often the source of life, for, without them mercy could not survive.

This river is the river of life. It is a living stream which nourishes our souls. In Psalm 1 we have a description of the blessed man who obeys the commandments of his God. He is like a tree planted by the rivers of water. His leaf shall not fade. His life is eternal. "I give unto them," says our Lord, "eternal life, and they shall never perish." This river which sustains our souls, and which, through the preaching of the everlasting Gospel, flows through the desert of this world flows from the throne of God and of the lamb. Those who thirst after God and His righteousness shall be abundantly satisfied by the river of His pleasure. In this life God's people sometimes dwell in a dry parched land; but the day is coming when they shall thirst no more. The river which sustained God's Israel in the wilderness had its source in the smitten rock; and it followed them to the end. Was this living stream not typical of Him from whose fulness all His people here receive grace for grace? This grace, or life, resides in Christ, the Rock of Ages. This grace is never, for a single moment, withdrawn from our soul. It is ever available and always sufficient. "My God shall supply all your need according to His riches in glory by Christ Jesus."

"Because of life the fountain pure
remains alone with Thee."

Rivers, as we know, also possess a purifying power. Those rivers that flow through the cities of the world and through many inhabited areas, bear away many of those things that would otherwise contaminate the air we breathe and damage our health. These impurities they carry away into the sea where they are dissolved. And the river of God's peace, which flows within our hearts, is one great source of our sanctification. Gently and quietly it is performing a work of holiness. What gave the Apostle John and Mary of Bethany that degree of holiness, and quiet composure of life, which some of their friends, failed to enjoy in the same measure? It was the peace of God which reigned in their hearts through their constant communion with their Lord. If Martha and Peter had kept His commandment to abide in His love in the measure in which they by His grace did, they would not have come under their Lord's rebuke. Whatever their distractions or temptations, their peace would also have been like a river.

And this is a peace which keeps our hearts and minds through Jesus Christ. What a lovely picture we get of King David in the third Psalm. Thousands were bent on his destruction, but on that night after he had crossed the brook Kedron he lay down in a quiet hollow deeply conscious of God's nearness and peace. The Eternal God was his refuge. He surrounded Him like a wall of fire. He feared no evil for God was beside him. And as he closed his eyes he was wrapped up in the great promises of another Psalm. "Because thou hast made the Lord, which is my refuge, even the Most High, thy habitation; there shall no evil befall thee, neither shall any plague come nigh thy dwelling." As God's preserving peace took possession of his soul he could say: "I will lay me down in peace, and sleep: for Thou, Lord, only makest me to dwell in safety."

Another mark of this peace is that it imparts joy to all who know it. "There is a river the streams whereof shall make glad the city of God." Those among us who belong to the Lord, and who have some measure of true Christian experience, may recall the day when this river just flowed through our soul. We might have been passing through great fears. Then we were brought into the desired haven of peace with God. We could then say that our joy was unspeakable. God's Word of peace was applied to our conscience and heart, so that we could sing with another

"That sacred stream, Thine Holy Word
That all our longing fears controls:
Sweet peace Thy promises afford,
And give new strength to fainting souls."

But what should give us the greatest joy in relation to this peace is that it is eternal. The sinful and deceptive peace of graceless men is momentary;

but this river is bearing God's people toward the ocean where God's peace shall be everlasting.

As long as we are in this world, however, our peace shall not be perfect. There are times when we are, in the words of Isaiah, tossed on the billows of affliction and without comfort.

In a Highland glen where I ministered for a few years, there is a river of great beauty, the waters of which are much varied in their flow. Here and there the river moves calmly through lovely meadows. And, in different places, there are large pools where the water is undistrubed. Then as we move along we hear and see a rumble of a flood in several places as the river dashes over precipitous rocks. Only where it touches its destination does this cease. So is our peace here. It varies with our days. And it shall so remain till we reach the place where our sun shall no more go down, and where our storms shall be changed into a calm.

> "Then are they glad, because at rest
> and quiet now they be:
> So to the haven He them brings,
> which they desired to see."

Let me say a word in conclusion on:

IV. The people who enjoy this peace

They are a people who hearken to God's commandments. When God brings us into a state of grace He opens our heart to hear and to obey His Word. We receive His statutes as our heritage for ever. In Psalm 119 we have, on the part of David, one prolonged prayer and holy resolve that he might be enabled by God's grace to keep the commandments of his God all his days. But this we cannot do unless we love Him. All His commands are summed up in the words, "Thou shalt love the Lord thy God with all thine heart, with all thy soul, with all thy strength and with all thy mind, and thy neighbour as thyself". "Love is the fulfilling of the Law." And before we love His law we must love Himself.

We may hear God's voice and yet not obey it. We may give formal assent that all His commandments are just and true while, on the other hand, we show in different ways that our hearts are destitute of His love. "I know you," said Christ, to the correct and, in their own eyes, perfect Pharisees of His day, "that the love of God is not in you."In their outward behaviour and cold carnal zeal for their own traditions, they were apparently faultless. But before the all-seeing eye of Christ, hatred filled their hearts. This all came to light when, without a cause, they crucified God's beloved Son. Love is the great imperative of God's kingdom. It is the very essence of God's nature, for "God is love". Whatever we do, whatever we are, without His love in our hearts we come to unending grief.

Are we not living in an age when this hatred of God and His Word is obvious to all who have any spiritual discernment? Not only out on the circumference of society, among the careless, the vandals and the degenerates may this be seen, but also within the so-called visible church. On all sides of us, and in many of our so-called "places of worship" are those who fail to proclaim the whole counsel of God, to respect His law, or to condemn the evils which are inevitably leading us to destruction. Apart from "the very small remnant" who are still to be found amoung us, one fears that we are the generation of His wrath.

Although the word "commandments" in this verse means the whole of God's infallible Word, it has a specific reference to the Ten Commandments which are God's unalterable moral law for all mankind. Within a brief space of time we have seen most of God's commandments, with the consent of many of our rulers and "leaders" in church and state, rejected, repudiated and disparaged. Such gross evils as Sabbath desecration, murder and immorality, now go unpunished or are condoned in our permissive society. But there is to be no place either in time or out of time for men who fail to hearken to God's voice. There is a limit to His forbearance. Soon, we fear, and unless we repent and return, He is coming out of His place to punish the inhabitants of the world for their iniquity.

God's appeal to us here, you will notice, is personal. Our ultimate relationship with God is awesomely personal. When a vessel is sinking, and the last bell is rung, it is "each man for himself". Try, dear unsaved friend, and let this thought take possession of your spirit. If you will not, the terrible torrents of Jordan will carry you one day to the Dead Sea of eternal darkness. O, that you would consider your latter end and that, through your acceptance of Christ, the river of God's peace would bear you on its bosom into the glorious land of uprightness.

At the beginning of my sermon I spoke about, "What might have been" both in our individual lives and historically in relation to Israel. With these words I would also end, giving them a personal application. Sit down, dear friend, and review your own life in the light of eternity. Ponder seriously on what might have been. The hour may be late, but do consider–"What may yet be" if you come to the One who "receiveth sinners" and Who is "waiting to be gracious".

God's greatest commandment with its promise to all of us is: "Believe on the Lord Jesus Christ and thou shalt be saved." On our response to this word our eternal destiny depends. Amen.